A Primer on
ECONOMIC GEOGRAPHY

A Primer on

The Primer series is under the editorial supervision of
PETER L. BERNSTEIN

ECONOMIC GEOGRAPHY

Robert B. McNee

RANDOM HOUSE *New York*

Copyright © 1971 by Random House Inc.
All rights reserved under International and
Pan-American Copyright Conventions.
Published in the United States by Random House, Inc.,
New York, and simultaneously in Canada by
Random House of Canada Limited, Toronto.

Library of Congress Catalog Card Number 74-124663

Standard Book Number: 394-31019-5
Manufactured in the United States of America.
Composed by H. Wolff Book Manufacturing Co.

First Edition

9 8 7 6 5 4 3 2 1

*For my wife,
Doris S. McNee*

Contents

PART I *Introduction* 1
   1 / General Introduction 3
   2 / Historical Perspective 15

PART II *Metropolis* 41
   3 / Services in the Metropolis 43
   4 / Manufacturing in the Metropolis 60
   5 / Primary Production in the Metropolis and Environs 76
   6 / The Metropolis as a Spatial Production System 91

PART III *The Metropolis Writ Large: The Economic Geography of Developed Countries* 105
   7 / Service Geography Beyond the Metropolis 107
   8 / Manufacturing Geography Beyond the Metropolis 125
   9 / Primary Production Beyond the Fringes of the Metropolis 149
   10 / Spatial Production Systems at the Supra-metropolitan Level 176

PART IV *The Underdeveloped World* 185
   11 / Locational Patterns in Underdeveloped Countries 187

BIBLIOGRAPHY 201

INDEX 205

PART I

Introduction

CHAPTER I

General Introduction

My grandmother was a tidy housekeeper. She believed in having "a place for everything and everything in its place." There may have been some logic behind the choosing of places to "put things" in her home, though the logic behind the locational pattern was not particularly obvious to visitors such as myself. No doubt she herself had forgotten the logic behind many of her locational choices. But what was more important was that the locational pattern was definite and unchanging. She always knew where everything was because she had memorized the precise location of everything in her home. And once having memorized a location she continued to use it, so that everything was very neat and very tidy and very simple.

Most of us are used to a kind of "grandmotherly" approach to economic geography. Of course economic geography deals with the location of production in a much larger home—the home of man, the earth. But the same memorizing approach has been traditional. For personal reasons, one memorized the location of one's house in relation to job, goods, education, recreation, and so on. For reasons of job mobility and good citizenship, one memorized the "principal facts" about the location of population, resources, farming, manufacturing, banking centers, trading centers, great cities, and so on. From childhood onward one gradually memorized the location of the fixed and unchanging features of man's earthly home, gradually built a mental map that was sufficient to guide one in making locational choices.

But whereas the location of things remained stable in my grandmother's home, it has hardly done so on man's home, the earth, during my lifetime. In the last half century, agricultural location has been transformed. Agricultural "belts," which used to be taught as fixed elements in the American pattern, have frequently shifted or dissolved. The so-called Cotton Belt of the Southeast is a good example. The Manufacturing Map of 1970 bears only partial resemblance to the Manufacturing Map of 1920. Where the *services* were located in 1920 did not seem all that important because only a relatively small percentage of people were employed in services, which were usually close to the farmers or factory workers. Thus, if one had memorized the map of farming and the map of manufacturing, one could guess at the location of services with a good chance of being right. But today more people are working in service functions than in any other and a great many of these services are tied only rather indirectly to farming or manufacturing locations.

Whole regions that were economically flourishing in 1900 or 1920 have become depressed economic areas (for example, Appalachia). Other regions of small population and supposedly limited potential have grown in population and economic production beyond anyone's dreams in 1900 (for example, Southern California). A vast movement of population to the cities, and especially to the great metropolitan areas, has transformed our whole way of life. There is still "a place for everything," but production has most certainly not stayed "in its place."

At the same time, our horizons have broadened. It was once thought sufficient to know the basic locational facts of one's hometown and, on a less detailed level, of one's country. One needed to know only the most general of "basic facts" about locations on the rest of the earth because contacts among nations were quite limited and individuals seldom traveled widely over the earth. But now the whole earth is very interdependent economically, and becoming increasingly so. And the chance that any one of us, as an individual, may be making locational choices about places almost anywhere on the earth is increasing rapidly. So memorizing becomes difficult. Grandmother could memorize the location of everything in her own home. But could she have memorized the location of everything in every apartment in New York City? Or even the location of every apartment in a city much smaller than New York? Memorization has its limitations.

In short, the traditional grandmotherly approach to economic geography is inadequate today for two reasons. First, it is inadequate because the location of production is so dynamic; our mental maps of "where things are" are always out of date, even if we are very avid students of economic geography. Second, this traditional approach is inadequate because the interdependence of the whole earth enlarges the list of locations we need to know to superhuman dimensions.

Yet the need to know economic geography—to know the locations of things relevant to production and livelihood—is greater than ever before. Increasing affluence gives us greater and greater mobility, but we cannot use this new freedom intelligently unless we understand the locational pattern of the earth and how and why it is changing. So there must be a better way than mere memorization of geographic patterns in the grandmotherly way.

Indeed, there is a better way than mere memorization of locational *facts*. We can search for locational *principles*, or the logic behind the myriad details of particular locational patterns. The growth of economic geography as a scholarly field—as opposed to grade-school geography, which has traditionally stressed the memorization of locational facts such as the principal products of places A to Z—is closely related to this search for logic and order in the observable patterns. Geographic scholars are trying to develop geometric and algebraic models that will be useful in generalizing about the location of production. Most of these models are specific to particular types of production. For example, the von Thunen model of agricultural location is not only highly useful in explaining some patterns of farming, but can also be used to explain some kinds of changes in these patterns. The various theories of manufacturing location do not explain everything about manufacturing by any means, but they most certainly help in bringing logical order to apparent geographic chaos. And in the various Central Place models there is the beginning of an explanation of the location of services.

Indeed, economic geography has come a long, long way since its first definition as a specific field of study in 1882. And it will probably develop a great deal further because the rapid locational changes of our time make the search for location theory very exciting for the scholar and very practical for the planner in government and the locational analyst in business. The principal ideas in some of the more widely accepted of these location models form one of the main threads of thought in this book. I have tried to explain such theories in simple language and to use them to give meaning to the specific geographic patterns the reader can observe around him or can learn about indirectly through the use of a good economic atlas.

But reliance on logic and theory should not blind us to their limitations. As noted above, the sweeping nature of locational change in our time is a powerful force in encouraging the development of location theory. Only a very few esoteric scholars would be interested in developing location theory if the location of production across the earth were as fixed and unchanging as the location of things in my grandmother's house. Because locations are very rapidly changing, the study of location is intellectually challenging and socially relevant.

Yet in such a time of rapid locational change, how can one be sure that a locational model developed from information collected for a particular place and time is valid for interpreting future locational patterns? To be of any great value over the long range, principles of location must be sufficiently comprehensive so that they will provide a guide to tomorrow as well as today and yesterday. Otherwise, memorizing locational models can be just as fruitless as the attempt to memorize the actual locational patterns themselves. Some aspects of present-day geographic location theory no doubt are timeless or, at least, will be of value throughout the lifetime of the reader of this book. But other aspects most certainly are already a bit archaic; they are less valid in explaining contemporary patterns than the patterns of 1920, and they may be of little but historic interest by the year 2000. Some of our hoary old theories should be retired from service right now, after having been duly thanked for years of faithful service. But, unfortunately, I cannot be sure which of them, though, of course, I have my prejudices.

Hence, the second great theme of this book, paralleling the stress on location theories, is the theme of locational revolution. I believe that, along with logical location theories, one needs a well-developed historical perspective if one is to make sense about contemporary geography. I believe that location theories can be highly useful if they are taken with a grain of salt, if one realizes that they are merely valiant efforts to understand a highly ephemeral situation. Trying to develop location theory in the twentieth century is a bit like trying to develop a theory of human behavior in Paris during the French Revolution. Depending on the month or year one studied the Parisians of the time, one could conclude almost anything about human behavior.

Chapter 2, "Historical Perspective," describes the contemporary changes in locational forces as the *Second Agglomerative Revolution*. Such changes began to find frequent geographic expression after about 1850; they seem to be gathering force since they have been more evident in recent decades than ever before. From the locational point of view, the single most important economic trend since 1850 has been a pronounced tendency toward agglomeration of production, toward the clustering of that which was formerly dispersed. Perhaps this is most obvious in the rise of the great metropolitan areas and the decline of the small towns and rural areas. But agriculture itself is agglomerating; so are many forms of manufacturing; and the rise of the suburban shopping center is only a special case in clustering. Even the widening breach between the so-called developed areas of the earth and the so-called underdeveloped areas is only a special form of the general tendency toward clustering of production.

I have manufactured the term Second Agglomerative Revolution in order to draw an analogy with the only other period in human history that seems similarly revolutionary from the geographic point of view. That is the period when man was first shifting from a very dispersed condition (hunting and gathering bands) to concentration in areas of agricultural potential and, within such areas, in villages, towns, and cities. That was the First Agglomerative Revolution. It began many millennia ago in a particular part of the earth—Mesopotamia, modern Iraq—and from there spread gradually over the earth. This new way of producing and of locating production was indeed a revolution and, as it spread, it transformed the economic geography of the earth in truly fundamental ways.

But after the initial transformation, basic locational changes were slower. In the late fifteenth century, when the Europeans began their advance over the earth, the Old World had reached a kind of locational equilibrium. It was a kind of grandmotherly world in which locational change was relatively slow. Perhaps there was a certain amount of disorder and "forgetfulness" as with a somewhat senile grandmother, but the basic geographic patterns were remarkably stable. And in that geographically stable age, we developed the habit of approaching geography as primarily a problem in the memorization of "facts" about places.

Of course, I know that my description of the Second Agglomerative Revolution is likely to be inaccurate in many respects. No one can know how long the contemporary locational fluidity will continue, nor what the most significant long-range locational forces will be, nor when, if ever, we will settle down again into some sort of locational equilibrium. After all, Alexis de Tocqueville's classic analysis of revolutionary France was written decades after that tumultuous period. But, inaccurate as my account must necessarily be, I think it provides a necessary background for the discussion of location theory in the chapters that follow. Further, it provides a point of departure for discussing these theories in dynamic terms. Hopefully, this approach will encourage the reader to think creatively about the economic geography observable around him, regardless of tradition or regardless of what location theorists say, or, for that matter what I say. For economic geography, as a coherent and relevant body of thought, is still very much unfinished business.

Having developed such a historical perspective, one can get on to the specific location theories dealing with agriculture, manufacturing, services, metropolitan areas, developed versus underdeveloped areas, and so on. But with which of these should one begin? Where should one start? Wherever one starts, the interpretation of economic location is always somewhat arbitrary because the economy as a whole forms a *system* of interrelated parts. It is obvious that the location of rural stores is not unrelated to the location of farmers and farming. Farming, in turn, is not located exclusively with relation to weather and climate and soil; it is related also to the location of the markets for its products, to the location of plants processing farm products, and to the location of ultimate consumers. And manufacturing is located where it is not only in relation to raw materials, labor, and markets, but also in relation to business services. Geographically, the economy forms a system, a vast, interrelated, locational web. Yet no matter how arbitrary it may be to start with only a small part of such a vast system, one does have to start somewhere. Which point of departure would be least arbitrary or most illuminating?

The classic approach in economic geography has been to start with the so-called *primary* forms of production: agriculture, forestry, mining, and fishing. From this one proceeds to the so-called *secondary* form of production: manufacturing, that is, processing and fabricating. So-called *tertiary* production, or services, is analyzed last of all. Since the services are particularly concentrated in cities, this means that the most pronounced feature of our contemporary economy, the metropolitan areas, is usually discussed last of all, as an addendum to the main inquiry. This approach has certain advantages. It is a *vertical* interpretation of production, stressing the flow of products or ideas upward or downward in the system. It reflects a hierarchical view of the social order that we have inherited from earlier times: peasants at the bottom, craftsmen a little higher, local storekeepers or professionals a bit higher, and the professionals in the capital city at the top of the pyramid.

It is comforting and reassuring to view the world in this

way, if one assumes one has a place in the upper part of the pyramid, however little such a view may actually reflect the world of today. It is advantageous, too, because it allows us to look at the whole earth from a single perspective. For the last several thousand years, the location of agriculture has been the single most powerful referent for the location of the economic system as a whole. Where there was farming there were also craftsmanship and services. Where agriculture was not, there were few services and little craftsmanship. The agricultural map provided the framework for the map of the economy as a whole. Even today, this is still largely true for much of the world's population. The great masses of people in China, India, Indonesia, Egypt, and many other areas are where they are primarily because of agricultural reasons. And the Second Agglomerative Revolution is so recent that the *inertia* of past locational patterns largely keyed to agriculture exerts a powerful control over contemporary patterns even in advanced economies such as those of the United States and Western Europe.

Furthermore, this approach is dear to map-lovers such as geographers, who like to explain as much about all areas of a map as possible. It is undeniably true that agriculture and forestry cover larger *areas* on economic maps than do manufacturing or services. If one's principal objective is to explain the use of the largest *areas,* then certainly agriculture should come first. In short, the classic pyramidal approach is a comfortable tradition, fits our prejudices, and allows us to view the earth in a simple, unified way.

However, this classic approach also has many disadvantages. The social order emerging in the advanced economies stresses social, economic, and political *equality* of all members of the production system rather than the pyramidal social structure of ages past. Farmers are no more "basic" to the American economy today than are plumbers, assembly line workers, school teachers, TV repairmen, or astronauts. And today, in advanced countries, the farmer behaves more like his urban cousin than he does like the contemporary peasant of Szechwan or his own ancestor of centuries past.

It makes little sense to view the earth in a single, unified way, if in fact the earth is more realistically viewed as having three parts: those to which neither the First nor Second Agglomerative Revolutions have come to any significant degree (places such as Antarctica), those organized according to the principles of the First Agglomerative Revolution and only partially affected as yet by the Second Agglomerative Revolution (places such as China, India, Egypt, Uganda, and Paraguay), and those places in which the Second Agglomerative Revolution originated or quickly came to, and hence places in which the Second Agglomerative Revolution is far advanced (places such as Western Europe, the United States, Australia, New Zealand, Canada, and, to a lesser extent, Eastern and Southern Europe).

Put differently, it makes little sense to analyze the whole earth in terms of norms that were highly appropriate to the First Agglomerative Revolution, including particularly the great emphasis on agriculture, when we are being moved locationally by forces of a different nature. Today, the location of the great metropolitan areas is much more crucial to the overall locational web of advanced countries than is the location of agriculture. Likewise, in a period of great locational fluidity, such as our own, it would seem to make more sense to stress that which is *changing* the locational mesh than to stress the *inertial* elements which are already passing into history. The great metropolitan areas are the single best example of the general agglomerative trend in the economy and they are also the central areas from which the rest of the economic map is being transformed.

The so-called underdeveloped areas of the earth differ from each other markedly in natural resources, population, and culture. They are similar to each other primarily in that they are *as yet* peripheral to the metropolitan economy; they have not yet been fully brought into the agglomerative system characterized by the modern metropolis. But that they will be so transformed ultimately seems likely (though I would not want to predict at what rate). Thus, at some time in the future, it may again be possible to view the earth's production mesh in a single, unified way, with a perspective based on an understanding of the locational forces released by the Second Agglomerative Revolution. But that time is not yet.

In short, I believe that a *horizontal* interpretation of the economic map is more rewarding than the classic *vertical* interpretation. In such a horizontal interpretation one does not start with the question of what is most "fundamental" or "basic" to the production process, as in the classic approach. Instead, one begins by asking what are the most central points on the economic map, the focal points from which the economy is organized and the generative points from which most of the new ideas affecting the economy flow to the ends of the earth. Unquestionably, these points are the great metropolitan areas.

This book is organized around the thesis that the great metropolitan areas are both the focus and the mirror of a modern economy. Chapters 3 through 6 discuss the location of production *within* metropolitan areas, the areas that already account for half or more of all production in advanced countries. Subsequent chapters in the book deal with production in the *metropolitan interstices*, the areas between metropolitan areas in advanced countries.

Chapter 3, the first of the metropolitan chapters, describes the location of *services* in the metropolis. Such a beginning is purposeful, in order to emphasize the large and growing role of services in a modern economy. Furthermore, the single most important area of a metropolis is primarily a service area, the Central Business District (downtown). Chapter 4, the second metropolitan chapter, analyzes manufacturing location within the metropolis and its environs. Chapter 5, the third metropolitan chapter, analyzes the forces that push primary production toward the fringes of the metropolis and the forces that tend to drive such production further away, into the metropolitan interstices. Chapter 6 is a summary chapter on the metropolis, an interpretation of the metropolis as a total locational system in which decisions affecting the location of services, manufacturing, and primary production are being made simultaneously rather than sequentially. This is one of the less satisfactory chapters because of the imperfect state of location theory. Although we recognize that the objective must be to understand the economy as a total system rather than only parts, the complexity of the whole system has as yet baffled most scholars.

Chapters 7 through 10 analyze the location of production within the metropolitan interstices of advanced countries and in other areas clearly tied to the metropolitan economy. Chapter 7 discusses services, again emphasizing the great importance of their location in a modern economy. Services are analyzed at two geographic levels. One level is the geometric pattern of services found in the hinterland of a metropolis. Another level is the pattern in which these service centers and the metropolitan areas of various sizes are themselves linked in a vast web of services extending over nations, supranational areas, and the developed world as a whole. Since I assume that the metropolis is indeed a mirror of the whole economy, but nevertheless an imperfect mirror, I have attempted to show how and why the location of such services is like or different from the pattern described in Chapter 3 for the metropolis. Similarly, Chapter 8 discusses the location of manufacturing beyond the individual metropolis, including manufacturing regions at a variety of levels. And Chapter 9 does similarly for agriculture and some other forms of primary production. Chapter 10 is analogous to Chapter 6; that is, it is a similar attempt to discuss developed economies as total systems rather than separate parts labeled services, manufacturing, or agriculture.

Thus, the bulk of the book, Chapters 3 through 10, forms an analysis of location in areas much affected by the Second Agglomerative Revolution. But what of the rest of the world? What about the countries still organized predominantly according to the norms of the First Agglomerative Revolution or those not yet modified much by either revolution? Although much can be said about the economic geography of such countries, most of this is detail along the lines of traditional grandmotherly geography. There are relatively few broad generalizations one can make about such countries as a group, except the obvious. Most generalizations tend to be comparisons with countries that are more developed, that is, more modified by the Second Agglomerative Revolution.

Hence, only one chapter, Chapter 11, is devoted to the so-called underdeveloped world, even though underdeveloped countries account for large portions of the earth's surface and large percentages of the earth's contemporary population. This may seem an unbalanced presentation, but economic geography is about the location of production. And most of the world's production is concentrated in the areas affected strongly by the Second Agglomerative Revolution.

It is my hope that throughout the reading of this book the reader will use his own direct observations and one or more modern economic atlases to check the validity of the locational ideas discussed here. The stress on the metropolis that runs through the whole book should help in this, since most readers are likely to be living in a metropolitan area. Hopefully, some reader of this book will have the eyes to see and the mind to interpret the locational revolution of our time. Hopefully, he will have an inquiring mind so that he can go beyond what is presented here to unravel some of the more significant locational riddles of today. The study of economic location has just begun and we economic geographers need all the help we can get.

CHAPTER 2

Historical Perspective

We are living in the midst of a profound locational revolution. The economic geography of the earth is changing in fundamental ways. Old locational patterns that endured for centuries are dissolving; new patterns are emerging to take their place. In observing contemporary economic geography, we cannot be sure whether the geographic patterns we are observing today are the shape of the future or whether they merely reflect either archaic locational patterns or temporary stages in the evolution of future geographic patterns now beyond our imaginings. Therefore, if we are to make sense of what we can observe around us, we need to develop some historical perspective about locational changes.

How far back in the economic geography of the earth must we look to gain the necessary perspective? Looking back a century, to 1870, provides some perspective. Though the populations of the economically advanced countries had already begun to concentrate in great metropolitan areas, most production was still widely dispersed. Economic geography perforce had a strong rural bias in those days. Today, in advanced countries, most production is highly concentrated in a small number of very large metropolitan and megalopolitan areas. (A megalopolitan area results from the gradual fusing of many metropolitan areas located close together, as on the Atlantic Seaboard of the United States.) Only a minor portion of their total production is in rural areas. Looking back two centuries, to the eve of the American Revolution, adds more perspective. How tiny the coastal cities of those days, such as New York or Philadelphia, seem in relation to the great urban centers of today. How different the modes of production; how dispersed and locally oriented production was. How slow the effects of new production in one place on the existing production in other places. Or, we could look back much further, to the economic geography of the earth before the great European voyages of discovery in the fifteenth and sixteenth centuries. How different the locations of production when the world was not yet economically one, when the most productive areas—China, India, the Middle East, Europe, and the Inca Empire—had little connection with each other.

But to really gain perspective on the locational revolution of our time one must go much further back, back to the dawn of civilization in Mesopotamia approximately 10,000 years ago. It was there and then that agriculture—as opposed to mere hunting and gathering—began. And it was there, a few millennia later, that the first cities arose. Obviously, the coming of agriculture and urbanism represented a truly fundamental change from the preceding economic geography of the earth. I am not a historian and I am not particularly interested in history for its own sake. But I believe that one has to look back that far, to the Mesopotamia of about five thousand to ten thousand years ago, to find a time when locational change in production was as pervasively revolutionary as that of our own time. In short, this chapter highlights the locational changes of today by comparing and contrasting them with a similarly revolutionary period, that of the Mesopotamian locational revolution.

Only a very brief sketch of the earth's economic geography before the Mesopotamian changes is needed as a baseline. The locational trials and tribulations of early societies were considerable, but they need not concern us greatly here except to highlight the sweeping nature of the Mesopotamian revolution, or the First Agglomerative Revolution. The population of the earth at that time was not only small, but it was very widely dispersed in small groups and bands. Why so small and so dispersed? Because the hunting and gathering economy generally could not concentrate enough livelihood materials at any one geographic location. Dispersal was a necessity for survival.

The population supporting capacity of most areas was distinctly limited with such an economy. Of course some rudimentary clustering of people must have occurred in especially favorable areas, but generally such clusters were limited to family groups or small tribal bands. That clustering of any kind occurred is economically and locationally significant because it allowed some rudimentary *division of labor*. The division of labor—occupational specialization—is one of the principal keys to all economic differentiation, including variations in the location of production.

At some point, perhaps about ten thousand years ago, there was a change. There was a change in the locational rules, the context of ideas within which locational decisions were made. Economic dependence on hunting and gathering gave way to dependence on agriculture and herding. Mankind began to agglomerate, to cluster together, much more than before. And the criteria used to decide which areas were most favorable and which least favorable for man changed. Now susceptibility to agricultural development became the principal criterion. Within the agricultural areas, further clustering occurred; hamlets and villages arose. Expanding opportunities for occupational specialization allowed some of the settlements to become larger than others.

By about 5,500 years ago, there were cities. Though these first cities had only a few thousand people rather than the millions we associate with a large city or metropolis today, they performed many of the same economic functions. This locational linkage between agriculture and the city, a new type of economy involving much more agglomeration than before, began at a particular place on the earth, Mesopotamia. From there it spread outward over the earth. As this agglomerative system spread, it transformed the economy, the locational pattern of production, and even the surface of the earth —through modifications of soils, land forms, vegetation, and animal life—over much of our planet. One might well ask, why? Why in Mesopotamia? Why were the locational rules now so different?

No one really knows just why the new locational pattern began in Mesopotamia rather than in some other place on the surface of the earth. No one knows why this particular place, over all others, was particularly fitted to become the birthplace of a set of ideas that transformed the earth. Of course, there is an abundance of conjecture, but that need not concern us here. It is much more important to consider the second question: why were the locational rules now so different?

One could answer simply that what I am talking about is the "rise of civilization." But that term has been used in so many ways and has so many meanings that it needs to be reworked if one is to use it effectively in geographic thinking. More specifically, what I am talking about is the rise of a new technology. But the concept of technology itself must be put in a geographic framework if it is to be of use to us here.

From a geographic point of view, it is useful to think in terms of *resource-converting techniques* and *space-adjusting techniques*. Resource conversion is man's modification of some earthly thing to adapt it to his purposes. In ancient Mesopotamia, this included the conversion of sunlight to edible grains through grain farming, the making of tools, and the like. It also included the modification of the surface of the earth itself, as with the clearing of land, the development of irrigation systems, and so on. Resource conversion today includes these things and many more, such as the chemical manipulation of petroleum derivatives to produce artificial rubber.

But merely modifying an earthly thing meets only part of man's need. Man also needs a *space-adjusting technology*, some means of getting the earthly thing from where it initially is to where he wants it to be. He needs means of overcoming the *friction of distance;* in other words, he needs the various forms of transportation, communication, packaging, and storage. And if he is to operate, as he must, over the space on the surface of the earth, he needs means of comprehending and controlling that space, as with maps, sketches, surveys, and land records. Today, while our space-adjusting technology includes improvements in transportation, it also, and more importantly, includes further improvements in interpreting space, as through satellite photography and computer mapping.

Most readers of this book are likely to be familiar, at least to some degree, with the advances in resource conversion and space adjustment that occurred in the ancient Middle East. Of course, all of them did not occur at once. Rather, they occurred over several millennia. Nor did all of them necessarily originate in Mesopotamia itself. But apparently Mesopotamia was the nucleus for the combination of ideas that was subsequently elaborated. Our concern here is to stress that a profound technological change did occur and that it provided the basis for a new economic geography.

From the geographic point of view, the most important thing about these changes in resource-converting and space-adjusting technology was that they were locationally agglomerative. They promoted the clustering together of population and production that were formerly dispersed. The agglomeration occurred on two geographic levels or scales. On the more general level, what occurred was a concentration of much of the population in particular kinds of areas, those amenable to agriculture and so developed. Other areas remained more thinly peopled. Thenceforth variations in density of population from place to place on the earth became a very important aspect of the emerging economic geography, probably more important than before. To this day, variations in population density related to agricultural potential remain a very important aspect of the interpretation of the economic geography of the earth.

But the agglomerative trend involved more than that. It involved also a tendency for the agricultural peoples to concentrate residentially in agricultural hamlets or villages rather than dispersing themselves over the land. Though the initial agglomerations of this type must have been small, they probably were larger than most of the permanent human centers that had ever existed before. The long process of concentrating people in larger and larger agglomerations had begun.

This process has continued to the present, so that we now have huge agglomerations such as Metropolitan New York (about seventeen million people). However, to have agglomerations of such great size, another locational revolution was necessary. This Second Agglomerative Revolution, which occurred much later, is discussed subsequently in this chapter.

The increased production from the land through agriculture permitted more people to be supported from it, and hence permitted agglomeration in villages. But permission is not the same as a requirement. Why did the people concentrate in hamlets and villages? No doubt there were many reasons, including military security, social needs, culture, and so on. But, clearly, there were economic advantages in agglomeration. Such concentration favored communication, cooperation, and exchange among the villagers. The existing division of labor could be much elaborated. Though the overwhelming proportion of the villagers were engaged in farming, some could become specialists in crafts—potters, weavers, blacksmiths—or services—selling, teaching, fighting, governing, performing rituals. Such elaboration of the division of labor increased the overall productivity of the village community. Hence more people could be supported from the land and the agglomeration could grow more populous.

The village became the chief agglomerative unit not only in the sense of the residence of the population, but also in the sense of a *focus* for the productive zone around it. Focality or centrality in economic geography became more important than before. The same principle of focality is still one of the keys to understanding economic geography today. Of course today the number of ways in which focality is expressed and in which it affects the map of production has been much elaborated. For example, focality today means one thing in the context of the metropolis—the focal role of downtown areas—and something else at the world level—the role of Chicago as a major center for air routes.

At some point, the villages became large enough so that rudimentary *economies-of-scale* emerged. Economies-of-scale involve a lowering of production costs per unit produced as a result of increasing the total output from the facility, generally through using the facility more completely and more continuously. Today we are very conscious of the importance of such economies, as with the reduction in prices that has generally accompanied the substitution of a large supermarket for the many small mom-and-pop groceries of the past, or reductions associated with the mass production of automobiles. Though the economies-of-scale that were possible in the villages of ancient Mesopotamia were modest in relation to those associated with mass production today, the principle is the same. Economies-of-scale were possible in bread making, brick making, grain storing, and the like. Such economies further enhanced the population-supporting capacity of the land and allowed the agglomeration to grow larger.

But there were limits to agglomerative growth. The villages tended to grow only up to a certain size range and then to level off in population. New villages might be established at some distance and these, too, would grow, but only up to a certain point. Why was this? The upper limits of growth were set by three things: the productivity of the land (which reflected the resource-converting technology in use as well as natural land qualities), the ease with which spatial friction could be overcome and hence the possible size of the focal zone tributary to the village (a function of the space-adjusting technology in use), and the socioeconomic organization of the village community (the development of economies-of-scale and the elaboration of occupational specialization). As improvements occurred in any of these elements, the agglomeration could grow larger until it reached a new locational equilibrium.

One way to expand the system was to extend occupational specialization beyond a single community (the village) to several communities. A super-village (an incipient town or city) might have most of the characteristics of other villages, but in addition it might provide special services (such as military protection or religious leadership or what we would now call wholesaling) or handicrafts to the other villages around it. A hierarchical pattern of communities might emerge, with economic advantages accruing from the concentration of certain more specialized activities in one central village. This would allow the central agglomeration to grow in population.

But if a two-step hierarchy is economically advantageous, why not hierarchies with three, four, or more steps in them? A super-village might serve several villages. In turn, a super-super-village might serve several super-villages and through them, the villages. Apparently, this was the economic rationale behind the great empires of ancient times and the explanation of the varying size of the capital city.

Apparently, the earth's first cities emerged in Mesopotamia. Though they were larger than mere hamlets or villages, their growth was limited not only by their military prowess, but also by the friction of distance. It is noteworthy that the more successful empires of ancient times put great stress on transportation, communication, and record keeping. Hierarchical agglomerative systems of the sort described could somewhat reduce the practical impact of the friction of distance, but they could not eliminate it.

Hierarchical agglomerative systems of the sort described prevailed over most of the agricultural areas of Eurasia until well into the nineteenth century. In Europe, in medieval times, there were generally at least three steps in the hierarchy: villages, towns, and cities. Villages were the same as described for Mesopotamia, though technological innovations over the centuries now permitted them to be larger than the initial ones. Towns were agricultural centers, like the villages, but in addition they were trading centers for several villages and they had greater handicraft development than most villages. Cities had the characteristics of villages and towns, but in addition they were administrative centers for religion, government, and military activity.

In 1500 A.D., broadly similar agglomerative patterns were found in many places beyond Mesopotamia. Were such patters of economic geography developed independently in these various places? Or were they the result of the outward spread of the resource-converting and space-adjusting technology of Mesopotamia? Of course, we cannot be sure. But apparently all of the other developments began later than those of Mesopotamia. And the places nearer to Mesopotamia seem to have had such development sooner than the countries farther away. This strongly suggests that a process of cultural diffusion was at work.

It appears that the first "cities," and the agricultural base on which they depended, had emerged in Mesopotamia by at least 5,500 years ago, perhaps earlier. Egypt, a little over 1,000 miles to the southwest, had cities by 5,000 years ago. West Pakistan, a little farther to the southeast, had cities by 4,500 years ago. And the other parts of the Indian subcontinent somewhat later than that. The Wei Ho Valley of northern China had agriculture and cities by 3,500 years ago; this is considerably farther east from Mesopotamia. Apparently, a Chinese version of the Mesopotamian agglomerative system spread eastward into the Yellow Plain from the Wei Ho Valley, then southward into southern China and on into Southeast Asia (where it met and mingled with an Indian version of the Mesopotamian agglomerative system). Simultaneously, the agglomerative revolution spread northeastward from northern China to Korea and Japan.

Meanwhile, the Mesopotamian agglomerative system was spreading westward and northwestward from Mesopotamia to Greece and, later, central Italy. The "civilization" carried northward in Europe by the Romans involved still another version of the Mesopotamian system. In the Middle Ages, the system continued to spread in Europe, especially northward and northeastward. The Baltic lands and northwestern Russia began to be strongly patterned in this fashion by about 1,000 years ago. Meanwhile, this agglomerative system was also spreading southwestward from Mesopotamia into Africa. Here, however, its progress was uneven, partly because of the large areas relatively unsuited to agriculture.

Of course, the movement of ideas about production is more complex than such a brief discussion suggests. Though Mesopotamia was apparently the initial point of origin for the basic set of ideas, elaborations on these ideas occurred in many places, including the more peripheral areas such as China. Such elaborative ideas were also diffused through the "known world." No doubt the reader is familiar with many of these subsequent technological innovations. However, it is very important to note that these technological advances were not locationally revolutionary in the same fundamental sense that the initial Mesopotamian advances were. Agglomerative systems expanded in geographic scope and increased in total population; and the cities at the top of the various hierarchies grew larger. But the fundamental patterns of economic geography remained unchanged. For example, various improvements allowed some imperial cities to be much larger than the early cities of Mesopotamia. Rome may have had 300,000 people at its height. But this was very unusual. Most cities and towns were much smaller, and all rested on an agricultural base, nearly always a village agricultural base.

By the time of Columbus and Vasco da Gama in the late fifteenth century, most of the known world had reached a kind of locational equilibrium. Though individual villages, towns, or cities might rise or fall in accordance with successes (such as military victories or commercial triumphs) or disasters (such as floods, droughts, plagues, or military defeats), the overall locational pattern had great stability.

It was this kind of locationally stable world that Malthus had in mind when he wrote his famous treatise on population, in which he asserted that population growth always tends to outrun growth in food production. Ironically, he wrote it at about the time this locationally stable world was beginning to pass away. For over a century, we have been living in a much more locationally flexible world, the world of the Second Agglomerative Revolution. The ideas of Malthus still apply in some force to the so-called underdeveloped world, to those parts of the earth not yet transformed by this second locational revolution. And, in the long run, ideas similar to those of Malthus may apply again everywhere. But not until this Second Agglomerative Revolution has run its course and a new locational equilibrium has emerged.

What is the nature of this Second Agglomerative Revolution? And what caused it? Before considering such questions, I must deal with a transitional period preceding it. The reality of the Second Agglomerative Revolution began to be obvious from about 1850 onward, perhaps earlier. The four centuries from about 1450 to about 1850 were a transitional period in a locational sense. Though the intellectual roots of modern science and technology are very old, it was particularly in this transitional period that modern science and technology were being developed to the point at which they would begin to markedly transform the earth after about 1850. These transitional years laid the groundwork, as it were, for the Second Agglomerative Revolution of our time.

Yet, at the same time, the period from about 1450 to about 1850 was the period during which the last great geographic advance of the First Agglomerative Revolution occurred. The world became one through the exploration, colonization, and conquest of the Western Europeans. As the Western Europeans moved over the earth, they sought to re-create everywhere the locational pattern with which they were familiar in their homelands, a variation on the Mesopotamian agglomerative system.

In some parts of the earth explored by the Europeans, they found that the First Agglomerative Revolution had preceded them. Of course this was true in Asia and in parts of Africa south of the Sahara, such as western Africa. But also in parts of America, particularly in Mexico, Central America, and Andean South America. There, they found a locational pattern of production that was analogous to that of their homelands. Though the resource-converting technology was not identical (for example, the major grain crop was maize, and horses, cattle, and sheep were unknown) yet the pattern had many similarities. The space-adjusting technology also differed in details. For example, though the Aztecs had carts, they apparently used them only as toys, not as key elements in production.

But the technology and the locational pattern of production had strong similarities that outweighed the differences. For example, the population was strongly agglomerated in agricultural zones. And within these, there was further agglomeration in villages, towns, and cities. Town planning, road building, storage, terracing, and the like had been much elaborated. Is it possible that in some obscure way Mesopotamian ideas had preceded the Europeans? We do not know. But, in any case, the coming of the Europeans to such areas meant changes in locational patterns, but changes much less sweeping than those where nothing resembling the First Agglomerative Revolution had been before.

Elsewhere, Europeanization generally meant the first arrival of anything closely resembling the locational patterns of Mesopotamia. True, *some* elements of that pattern, such as rudimentary agriculture, predated the arrival of the Europeans in parts of America, southern Africa, and so on. But, generally, the locational linkage between a highly developed agriculture and a hierarchical agglomerative pattern of hamlets, villages, towns, and cities had not yet emerged. Through Europeanization the agriculturally suitable areas of North America, eastern South America, southern Africa, Australia, and New Zealand were transformed to fit patterns developed millennia before in Mesopotamia.

In relation to the long millennia it took for Mesopotamian ideas to spread across Eurasia, this Europeanization was very rapid. The rapidity and ease of the European advance allowed some locationally significant variations on the traditional themes. For example, the farmers in North America often settled in a dispersed pattern on the land rather than residentially concentrating in agricultural villages. Hence, the hamlets and villages of rural areas of this type were really more like the historic European town than they were like the historic European village, which was first and foremost a residential site for farmers.

The overall locational system of the earth was modified in the process of European expansion in another way, too. The economic unification of the earth and improvements in space-adjusting technology (especially the sailing ship) allowed an elaboration of the historic hamlet-village-town-city agglomerative hierarchy. Such spatial systems could now be much larger in geographic scope, with more hierarchical layers or levels, and the population center at the top of such a hierarchy could be more populous. The capital cities and port cities of Europe grew larger than any preceding agglomerations.

By 1800 London had over one million people, apparently the first agglomeration to attain that size. But though the economic functions of London were broadly similar to those

Historical Perspective / 27

of the early imperial capitals of the Middle East, there is some question as to whether or not one can meaningfully apply the same general term, city, to both. The great difference in the size of the agglomeration really meant a new kind of agglomeration. London was more than a mere city; it was a metropolis. As a metropolis, it heralded the new age of the Second Agglomerative Revolution. For during the next century and a half, the metropolis became commonplace, the "norm" in so-called developed areas rather than the special case. And the metropolis became symbolic of a whole series of locational changes suggested by the term Second Agglomerative Revolution.

Hypothetically, the earth might have settled down into a new locational equilibrium after the European global advance, an equilibrium based on the final global triumph of the First Agglomerative Revolution. But it did not. Why not? Because a modern science and a modern technology arose that had quite different locational implications. Since modern science and technology have not yet run their course, we cannot know what all of those implications will be. But it is possible to note some of those that apparently have been of importance so far.

The rise of science as a system of belief, with an accompanying decline in belief in supernaturalism and magic, seems particularly important. Perhaps man has always yearned to conquer and control his environment, who knows? But in the past, the stress was on adjusting and conforming to the earth rather than conquering and controlling it. Today, belief in science and technology encourages men to expect that all of their wishes about conquest and control of their environment can be granted. And granted quickly, in our time, not in some far future time. As a consequence, the old locational patterns are being called into question.

The technological changes of our time have been described many times by many authors. In particular, the term Industrial Revolution is often used. But, in addition, all sorts of other revolutions have been described: the agricultural revolution, the mineral revolution, the mechanical revolution, the electrical revolution, the chemical revolution, the cybernetic revolution, and so on. And on. Such terms have their uses in particular contexts. But in a geographic context, such terms are too restrictive. To understand contemporary economic geography—the locational pattern of production—one needs a more comprehensive term. And a term more suggestive of the dominant locational element in the change, agglomeration. That is why I use the term Second Agglomerative Revolution. But before getting into the specific locational changes occurring, I want to discuss the changes in resource-converting technology and space-adjusting technology that permit this new locational fluidity and agglomeration.

In the last century or so there has been a quantum leap in our ability to modify the surface of the earth for our purposes. Increasingly, man shapes the geometry of the earth's surface to his will, rather than modifying his expectations in deference to an unyielding earth. Forests were once a real obstacle to the spread of agriculture. Supernaturalism and magic associated with trees sometimes stayed men's hands. But, in any case, the woodcutting tools available before the nineteenth century permitted only a slow and gradual advance into forested lands. Today forests are a resource rather than an obstacle and their locations are adjusted to fit preconceived geometries rather than having the locational pattern of the economy as a whole adjusted to fit forest boundaries.

So, for grasslands. The thick sod of prairie lands was a real obstacle to the simple plows developed in the ancient Middle East and carried around the world by the First Agglomerative Revolution. But no sod can withstand modern plowing equipment. Irrigation is a very old art; the agriculture of the Middle East has owed much to the perfection of this art almost from the beginning. But water technology today, including scientific methods of converting salt water to fresh water, is of a different order of things from those ancient ways. Similarly, the available technology for physically and chemically manipulating soils is of a quite different dimension than the slower and less effective techniques of soil modification developed in the long centuries since agriculture began in Mesopotamia.

The revolution in earth-moving equipment, symbolized by

the bulldozer, but actually involving a large number of engineering advances in the last century, is reshaping the land. Industrial man is an earth sculptor. Part of this has come because the Second Agglomerative Revolution is conspicuously a "mineral revolution." Dozens and perhaps hundreds of minerals mined today in large volume were hardly considered resources at all in 1850, such minerals as petroleum, aluminum, magnesium, titanium, and radium. The advance of the First Agglomerative Revolution was keyed to demands for food; the advance of the Second Agglomerative Revolution is keyed to minerals at least as much and perhaps far more. The susceptibility of an area to mining development is now an important locational referent paralleling the historic one of agriculture.

But earth-moving equipment is also highly important in many other aspects of modern life—in highway building, city building, and so on. Millions of acres of the earth's surface have been transformed and millions more are being transformed for mining purposes or to make the irregularities of the surface conform to architectural or engineering blueprints produced far from the site being modified. More and more, the locational patterns in men's minds are more crucial in creating economic geography than the actual shape of the earth itself. The patterns in men's minds are highly generalized and simplified in comparison to the immense variety of the unmodified earth.

Paralleling such changes, there have been changes in the direct production process itself. Much has been made of the *mechanical* changes, as is implied in the usual stress on the role of machines in the Industrial Revolution. Indeed, mechanization, a form of applied physics, has been of great importance. But applied chemistry and biology have been highly important too. For example, the accelerating productivity of contemporary agriculture owes as much or more to new crops, new ways of raising animals, new insecticides, new herbicides, new fertilizers, and so on, than it does to mechanization alone. And, of course, the marked growth of population in our time has resulted primarily from applied chemistry and biology, innovations in medicine and hygiene.

The effect of such changes on the patterns of economic geography has occurred particularly through occupational shifts, with a resultant loosening of the former constraints on agglomeration. As the technology improved, there has been a steady decline in the percentage of all workers employed in primary economic activity (agriculture, grazing, forestry, mining, and fishing). For a time, this resulted in a marked increase in the percentage of all workers in secondary economic activity (manufacturing) and a less marked increase in the percentage in tertiary economic activity (services). But as the technology has improved further, the percentage of workers in manufacturing has declined, too. Therefore, in terms of numbers of people employed, the economies of advanced countries are more and more "service economies."

Meanwhile, technology is also eating away at opportunities for service employment of the more routine sort. For example, machine vending displaces sales personnel. Or, wrinkle-free clothing displaces the ironer, and so on. So a higher and higher proportion of all service employment is in categories requiring advanced education, continuing education to keep abreast of innovations, frequent consultation with other experts, and the exercise of judgment as well as the application of routine knowledge. Examples include research positions and the higher-level bureaucratic jobs of government and private firms. This aspect of services has now become important enough that some authors think it should be given a separate designation to distinguish it from the more routine services. They call it "quaternary economic production." For the foreseeable future, this quaternary production will grow in employment significance more rapidly than either primary or secondary production and perhaps even more rapidly than tertiary production.

As noted earlier in this chapter, the historic hamlet-village-town-city agglomerative hierarchy was an expression of a particular division of labor. It was a compromise solution to a locational dilemma. On the one hand, survival required a highly dispersed economy because the base of the economy was agriculture. Agricultural production was necessarily dispersed because the raising of crops is essentially the harvesting of sunlight, and sunlight is indeed dispersed. But on the other hand, there were economic advantages in agglomeration, advantages of occupational specialization and also rudimentary economies-of-scale. The historic agglomerative hierarchy was an uneasy compromise, permitting a few of the advantages of agglomeration while retaining the benefits of dispersal.

But today, the more agricultural employment declines in relation to total employment, the more the historic constraints on agglomeration become insignificant. It is not just that more of the population can now live in towns or cities rather than in hamlets or villages. No, indeed. It is that a new form of agglomeration can emerge, the giant metropolis of millions of people or the giant megalopolis of tens of millions of people. Since such agglomerations grow in relation to their own internal economic natures more than they do in relation to an agricultural hinterland, we do not yet know what the economic limits to the size of such agglomerations actually are.

They grow because there are real economic advantages in concentrating most forms of secondary, tertiary, and quaternary production. And they will continue to grow until the disadvantages of such concentration (problems of pollution, congestion, social disorganization, and so on) clearly outweigh the advantages. The removal of the old constraints on agglomeration has been very sudden in terms of the long history of mankind. Mankind is now engaged in an exciting voyage into the unknown future, a voyage to discover what the most advantageous new agglomerative pattern should be.

But it is not only that all occupations other than those related to primary production have been agglomerating. Here, too, there are important forces of agglomeration at work. In advanced countries, agriculture is becoming less and less dispersed. It is becoming more and more concentrated in especially favorable zones with many uncultivated areas in between. And specific types of agriculture, such as the raising of a particular crop or a particular animal, are becoming more and more concentrated in highly specialized zones or regions. Similarly, whereas the mining of past centuries was done generally at a great many widely dispersed sites, mining is highly concentrated today in a relatively few places at which mass production techniques can be used. In short, the process of agglomeration is a general one, affecting every type of employment and every aspect of the economy.

Of course, this agglomerative revolution owes much to innovations in space-adjusting technology as well as in resource-converting technology. Popular literature tends to stress the great importance of the new technology's *speed*. The contrast of the jet and the oxcart is a vivid one indeed. But, locationally, speed is only one aspect of the change. Locationally, the economies-of-scale involved in modern mass transport are probably much more important. Such economies permit us to move bulk products of low per-unit value over great distances at low cost. On the one hand, this permits such great agglomerations as Metropolitan New York to develop; products can be brought to New York from great distances at relatively low cost, a cost less than the economies achieved by concentrating the manufacturing and services of New York in such an agglomeration. On the other hand, economies-of-scale in transportation permit agglomeration in primary production, too. Specialized agricultural regions such as the Wheat Belt would have been inconceivable before the railroads and modern shipping.

But innovations in space-adjusting technology involve much more than the familiar changes in transportation and communication. Improvements in packaging and storage are as important in their way as improvements in the actual means of transportation. The most significant architectural innovation of the new age, the skyscraper, rests in turn on many technical ideas—the development of cheap steel, the idea of curtain-wall buildings, the idea of the elevator, and so on. Who can conceive of a modern metropolis without the skyscraper, the epitome of agglomeration in human activities! Then, too, there have been many innovations in the means of interpreting and controlling space, such as modern mapping, aerial photography, satellite photography, computer mapping, new census methods, and more sophisticated techniques for regional planning.

The locational pattern of the earth will remain unstable as long as locationally significant innovations in resource-converting and space-adjusting technology keep coming. A new locational equilibrium, like that which prevailed in the known world in 1450, cannot develop unless such technological innovation slows down and stops. How long will we maintain our pace of technological change? No one knows. But advanced economies today put great stress on "research and development." That is, they use part of the production surplus to finance further technological innovation. Perhaps this is one of the major reasons that technological change is so much more rapid in our time than in centuries past. This suggests that the locational pattern might never stabilize.

However, not all innovations are locationally significant, and some are more locationally significant than others. Though there were significant technological changes in the long centuries after the First Agglomerative Revolution began in Mesopotamia, these innovations were generally not locationally revolutionary in the same sense that the initial Mesopotamian developments were. So the contemporary fluidity in the patterns of economic geography may change to stability at some time in the future.

Thus, the locational rules, the context within which locational decisions are made, have changed in our time. These rules are quite different from those that have prevailed over much of the earth since the coming of the Mesopotamian locational revolution. Where did this Second Agglomerative Revolution begin? How far has it spread over the earth? How long will it take to reorder the economic geography of the whole earth?

The point of origin, or culture hearth, for the new economic geography was a small zone in western Europe not much larger than Mesopotamia: England, Scotland, the Low Countries, and the Rhine zone of France, Germany, and Switzerland. It was there that most of the rudimentary inventions and discoveries so important in the Second Agglomerative Revolution first occurred. These developments first occurred during the locationally transitional period from about 1450 to 1850. Their expression in the geographic landscape was minor until about 1850, though they were there, obscured by the historic locational patterns. Of course, many of the ideas that emerged in that small zone in western Europe had historical origins in other parts of Europe (such as central and northern Italy during the Renaissance) or in the Middle East. But it was from the North Sea zone that modern science and technology emerged to transform the economic geography of the earth. The new ideas spread quickly in parts of western Europe adjacent to the North Sea zone and across the North Atlantic to America. So by the early nineteenth century or at least by 1850 the core of the Second Agglomerative Revolution was the North Atlantic Basin. From the Atlantic Seaboard of the United States and from western Europe the ideas of the Second Agglomerative Revolution have spread to large parts of the earth.

The geographic advance of the Second Agglomerative Revolution can be seen in many locational effects besides the most obvious one of the rise of huge agglomerations, the great metropolitan areas. It can also be seen in the rise of agglomerative trends *within* metropolitan areas, as with skyscrapers and Central Business Districts, large suburban shopping areas, manufacturing complexes, medical complexes, and so on. It can be seen in the interstitial areas between metropolitan areas in the form of the specialized production regions emerging in agriculture, forestry, and mining. It can be seen in the rise of specialized outdoor recreational areas, "escape hatches" for the harried but affluent inhabitants of the metropolis. It can be seen in the tendency to use the metropolitan areas as the major locational reference points for the whole locational mesh of the economic system rather than the land itself as the main reference point. It can be seen in the earth sculpturing of bulldozers and other instruments with which man now shapes the land to his will. It can be seen in the rise of locational planning at both the metropolitan level and the national level and can be heard in anguished cries about the "crisis of the cities" (really, largely the crisis of rapid metropolitanization). It can be seen in the much greater freedom of locational choice man now has and the ease with which choices are changed in some cases, such as mining. It can be seen in a general locational instability and flexibility.

It can be seen in the confusion of the people, learned scholars as well as ordinary citizens, as the locational patterns of agriculture no longer provide the matrix for the whole locational system as they have done since the dawn of civilization. Or the confusion of the people as the historic hamlet-village-town-city hierarchical agglomerative system declines in importance as a grid on which the economy can be hung. The cultural values that emerged over thousands of years under "civilization" (the Mesopotamian agglomerative system) presupposed a geographic pattern of production rooted in agriculture and this historic hierarchial occupational locational structure. Now, to some people, these values seem threatened. To them it seems that the whole world is becoming unhinged.

Within the North Atlantic Basin, most of these elements are present. Beyond, the pattern is more spotty. But generally, the economic geography of the so-called developed countries (including the United States, Canada, Europe, the Soviet Union, Japan, Australia, New Zealand, and some others) tends to be dominated by the new patterns, even though aspects of the First Agglomerative Revolution still survive and modify the total pattern. Some aspects of the Second Agglomerative Revolution are also found in the underdeveloped countries of Africa, Asia, and South America, but in a spotty and selective fashion so that there the patterns of the First Agglomerative Revolution are generally dominant and the new patterns only local variations on the main pattern.

The long-range geographic implications of the Second Agglomerative Revolution are somewhat obscured by the role of *locational inertia* in both developed and underdeveloped countries. According to the idea of inertia in physics, that which is at rest tends to remain at rest unless some new force is applied. So with the location of production. A geographic pattern of production, including the geometric relationships among all the places involved in the production network, tends to remain inert, to stabilize, unless there is a force to change it. The Second Agglomerative Revolution is a great economic force, but its effect is felt most acutely in areas previously rather undeveloped but now developing rapidly, such as the frontier zones.

In previously developed areas, though the Second Agglomerative Revolution has sufficient force to radically change the previous geometric pattern, some aspects of the earlier pattern may survive at least in diluted form for a time. For example, most of the large metropolitan areas of the developed world are in areas amenable to agricultural development, either now or in the past, even though such agricultural potential is no longer a prime locational referent for the growth of a metropolitan area. The Second Agglomerative Revolution began as an outgrowth of the First Agglomerative Revolution and that revolution's principal locational rule was a close geographic association of agriculture and urban development. Hence the location of the population at the beginning of the Second Agglomerative Revolution favored some continuation of this geographic association.

But it is clear that over time this kind of geographic association will wither in overall importance for world geography. This is clear because already there are many large metropolitan areas in the developed world that are rather marginal to the main agricultural zones, such areas as Miami, Tucson, Duluth-Superior, and the Siberian settlements. It is quite possible that, in the future, the prime locational referent for most metropolitan areas will be pleasant surroundings (scenic beauty, recreational opportunities, enjoyable climate, and so on) rather than the location of agriculture, mining, or similar considerations. It is important to remember that the Second Agglomerative Revolution is not much more than a century old and that its transformation of established geographic patterns has just begun. Today, the role of locational inertia is still great enough so that contemporary patterns in economic geography are a mixture of new and old, like one photograph superimposed on another.

In many places, the Second Agglomerative Revolution has outrun the First Agglomerative Revolution. Thus there are large parts of the earth—for example, the polar forest and tundra zones, the great deserts, some tropical forest areas, and many grassland areas—in which the First Agglomerative

Revolution made little permanent impact. But now the Second Agglomerative Revolution is transforming parts of such places, particularly in the search for mineral deposits amenable to mass production methods. Whether such places will be transformed ultimately by a full range of agglomerative developments or whether they will be influenced only by such selective aspects of the Second Agglomerative Revolution as mining agglomeration remains to be seen. Hypothetically at least, these initial penetrations of the frontier lands could become the nuclei for new agglomerative patterns at some future stage in the development of the Second Agglomerative Revolution.

Distance (spatial friction) and the hazards of pioneering in unfamiliar earthly environments were primary obstacles to the spread of the First Agglomerative Revolution. These factors are still operative and retard the spread of the ideas associated with the Second Agglomerative Revolution. Other things being equal, underdeveloped countries adjacent to developed countries are more likely to receive the new ideas repeatedly and with force than underdeveloped countries located farther away. And since the Second Agglomerative Revolution began in the North Atlantic Basin, scientific and technological knowledge applicable to that type of environment is still much advanced over such knowledge applicable to different environments, such as the humid tropics. For example, our knowledge about tropical diseases is quite limited in comparison with our knowledge of mid-latitude diseases. Similarly, our knowledge of soils and biology for the mid-latitude lands is much more extensive.

But perhaps the most important single obstacle to the spread of the ideas of the First Agglomerative Revolution was cultural resistance. The history of the Old World is replete with examples of peoples who resisted the ideas of the First Agglomerative Revolution, clinging to older locational patterns as long as they could, and still survive. And there are many examples of peoples who adopted parts of the Mesopotamian "locational package" while rejecting other parts. For example, the Celtic peoples of western Europe accepted some of the agricultural aspects of that revolution while rejecting the idea of the hamlet-village-town-city agglomerative hierarchy. They preferred a simple pattern involving hamlets and villages, but not towns and cities. But alien peoples in time forced the more complete agglomerative pattern on them. Similarly, many of the Berber peoples of northwest Africa have resisted the rise of the town and the city, preferring more flexible forms of agglomerating production, as with periodic fairs at open sites. A full history of such resistance to the spread of the First Agglomerative Revolution can never be written, because much of it went unrecorded. However, such as was recorded suggests that cultural resistance to change was at least as important as distance itself in retarding the spread of this agglomerative revolution.

And so it is today. People value that with which they are familar, including particular locational patterns of production. The United States has been a rather highly-urbanized country for some decades. Yet a poll of the American people would show a high percentage feel that a small town is a better place to live and rear children than the metropolis. Indeed, there is still a strong rural bias or anti-metropolitan bias in America, even as Americans move to metropolitan areas at a rapid rate. There is a general tendency to discuss the metropolis primarily in terms of its problems, rather than in a more comprehensive way that would include discussion of opportunities and economic advantages in the metropolis as well as problems. How can one explain the rapid growth of the new agglomerative system and the pervasive dissolution of the old agglomerative patterns unless there are distinct advantages in the new patterns?

Similar cultural resistance to the spread of the Second Agglomerative Revolution can be noted in other developed countries, such as Great Britain, the West European countries, and Japan. And if there is lingering resistance to the new locational patterns in those countries in which the revolution is so far advanced, of course we should not be surprised that many people in the underdeveloped countries view the new patterns as disruptive of all they hold dear. Since the strength of such cultural resistance is difficult to measure, it is difficult to predict at just what rate the revolution will continue to spread or how soon the patterns associated with it will become the dominant patterns everywhere, in all countries. However, it seems quite clear that the Second Agglomerative Revolution will continue to spread and that this spread is much more rapid than the spread of the First Agglomerative Revolution.

Though the cluster of ideas that generated the First Agglomerative Revolution developed in one area, ancient Mesopotamia, many ideas were gradually added to that cluster from places to which the revolution spread, such as China or Greece. It seems reasonable to assume that the same would hold true for the Second Agglomerative Revolution. At first, the countries outside the Atlantic Basin tended to be mere copiers of the new ideas without contributing much of a fundamental nature to them. But gradually some of those countries, such as Japan, have begun to make basic contributions to modern science and technology. So far, the *locational pattern* of the developed countries has not been affected very much by such ideas originating beyond the North Atlantic Basin. But the Second Agglomerative Revolution is still young. There is no reason to assume that in the future there may not be significant changes in the locational patterns of developed countries from locational innovations originating beyond the North Atlantic world. In the long run, such innovations may do more to change our locational patterns than our own research and development expenditures. The possibility of such cultural cross-pollination is a further reason for anticipating continuing locational flexibility and instability in our own time and far into the unknown future.

In short, we are living in the midst of a profound locational revolution. The reality of this revolution must be the context in which we set our attempts to develop theories and laws about the location of economic production.

PART II

Metropolis

CHAPTER 3

Services in the Metropolis

The metropolis has been the prototype of a modern, industrialized economy for over a century; it has been the most characteristic single expression of the Second Agglomerative Revolution. But whether it is a relatively permanent phenomenon or only a passing phase in that locational revolution, we do not know. For example, it may be that the most prominent feature of the economy in the coming century will be the "megalopolis," a great, sprawling concentration of people and production created by the gradual merging of many formerly separate metropolitan areas. After all, many of our metropolitan areas that now appear unified were once many separate villages, towns, and cities that happened to be located close together and happened to grow from general economic influences that affected the whole area. But today, the metropolis is still the best single laboratory in which to study locational processes that affect modern economies. Hence, in this chapter, and subsequent chapters, the metropolis is used as a mirror to interpret locational patterns of general interest in the economy.

The term *metropolis* or *metropolitan area* is a very broad term, including a great variety of urban agglomerations and a great variety of geographic patterns. For example, one expects a metropolis of many millions such as Chicago or New York to have more complex internal geographic patterns than a metropolis of only 100,000 people. One expects metropolitan areas that were already large before the automobile era began (for example, London, New York, Philadelphia, and Cincinnati) to differ in their internal patterns from those that developed largely after the coming of the automobile age (for example, Detroit, Houston, and Los Angeles). One expects a metropolis with clearly defined ghettos, such as Cleveland or Chicago, to have somewhat different internal patterns from a metropolis in which ghettos are minor or absent, such as Minneapolis, Minnesota or Milan, Italy. And so on. Size, age, and economic and cultural diversity make a great deal of difference. But my purpose here is to simplify, not to confuse by going into all of the complexities found in every metropolis. Therefore, the discussion in this and subsequent chapters is in terms of a hypothetical metropolis of medium size and average characteristics.

A Hypothetical Metropolis

For simplicity's sake, the metropolis being described here is assumed to have (1) a total population of about one million people, (2) a mixed economy, including well-developed services and well-developed manufacturing and a smattering of primary production (especially agriculture and mining) on its margins, (3) a diversified economy, including many kinds of manufacturing rather than only one or two, and many kinds of services provided for its hinterland rather than only a few, (4) opportunity to grow in all directions without restrictions imposed by major terrain barriers such as mountains, swamps, or canyons, (5) a well-developed and diversified transportation network with a major focus in the center, though not necessarily a completely radial pattern, (6) an inner portion reflecting particularly the building styles of the pre-World War II period and an outer portion reflecting particularly the building styles of recent decades, (7) moderate and sustained rates of growth in population and economic production, (8) a general tendency for the density of population to be greatest in the inner parts, in the zone surrounding the Central Business District, and to gradually decrease outward in all directions, and (9) sufficient social, economic, and cultural integration of the population so that variations in the ethnic patterns do not modify internal patterns to any marked degree.

The Pattern of Services: The General Case

A modern economy is a service economy, that is, there are more people employed in providing services than in any other type of economic activity. These services are of a great range and complexity, including retailing, wholesaling, and personal services such as dry cleaning and hair styling. They include the law, medicine, education, and so on. How can one generalize about the geographic or locational patterns of such a wide range of activities? The most ubiquitous services are retailing and the more common personal services such as barbering. So these will be discussed first. And these will be discussed in terms of their most common patterns first, with variations and contemporary trends discussed later.

In most Occidental economies, the customer is king. Stores tend to try to provide what the customer wants, including what the customer wants in terms of store location. But where do the customers want the stores to be? Being human, customers want many things and some of these are mutually contradictory. For example, most customers would like to have the stores as close to their homes as possible, in order to minimize the time and effort spent getting to and from the stores. Yet many customers also want a quiet, safe street on which to live and rear their children. So, there is a conflict between shopping convenience and the desire to live away from traffic. Similarly, there is a conflict between conveniences and low prices. Most customers want low prices for goods. Yet the prices charged by a store reflect its volume of business. Economies-of-scale can be great in a large store with rapid turnover of merchandise; these economies tend to be passed on to the consumer in order to attract still more consumers.

If economies-of-scale were to be fully realized in the metropolis, there would be only a few giant stores and no small neighborhood stores. But these giant stores would necessarily be quite distant from the homes of most of the people. Customers have still other wishes, too. Usually, they want the opportunity to choose items from among a great variety of sizes, shapes, colors, models, prices, and so on. Partly, this could be achieved in the giant stores. But different store managers have different ideas about what the customer might want. So a *cluster* of stores gives more real choice than a single giant store, in most cases. Likewise, the customer has other things to think about besides going to the store. He wants to be able to do most of his shopping on the basis of habit, without a careful weighing of the pros and cons of various store locations on every single shopping trip. He wants to be able to carry a highly simplified map of the retailing of the metropolis in his head, not a detailed blueprint. He has still other conflicting wishes, too—far too many to detail here. How can all of his conflicting wishes be granted; how can the stores locate according to where he wants them to be?

Conflicts are resolved by compromises. The retailing geography of the metropolis is a compromise. Like all compromises, it is subject to change as the differing desires that produced the conflict wax or wane in importance or as changes in income or technology permit a given desire to be realized more or less readily than before. Thus, the coming of the automobile did not eliminate the basic conflict between the desire for nearness (requiring many small stores) and the desire for low prices (requiring fewer and larger stores). But it changed the practical meaning of nearness. The pattern of many, many, small mom-and-pop groceries widely dispersed in every part of the metropolis shifted to a pattern of fewer groceries, larger in size, farther apart, with greater volume and turnover, and lower prices—the supermarket pattern of today. The coming of the automobile did not eliminate the conflict or the need to compromise; what it did was to alter the kind of geographic compromise necessary and possible. Nearness, as defined by most grocery shoppers, still means something less than traveling all the way across town. Otherwise, all grocery shopping would have become concentrated in the Central Business District or some other central point. Instead, supermarkets are found very widely distributed, but less widely than the small groceries of yesteryear.

For retailing and for the more common services in the metropolis today, the locational pattern is best understood in terms of a kind of scale. At one end of the scale are items for which nearness is very important in relation to price, variety, or other desires. Examples include milk, bread, cigarettes, and barber services. Such items are highly standardized in price and quality. They are also items that are purchased regularly and frequently. At the other end of the scale are items for which nearness is relatively less important than price, variety, and so on. Examples include imported caviar, wedding dresses, fur coats, and oil paintings. These are much less standardized in price and quality. And they are not purchased very frequently by most consumers. Between these two extremes, there are many variations in the relative importance of nearness versus other considerations. By tradition, those items for which nearness is the prime consideration are called *lower order* goods and services, and those at the opposite end of the scale are called *higher order* goods and services.

One would expect to find the lower order goods and services very widely distributed in the metropolis, and they are. They are found in the smaller neighborhood shopping areas, in the Central Business District, and in the shopping areas of medium size—what are usually called *regional* shopping areas. One would expect to find the highest order goods and services available at only a very few locations, perhaps only in the Central Business District. Or, perhaps, too, in a suburban shopping center if it were large enough to rival the CBD (Central Business District) itself. And one would expect to find the middle level goods and services (such as major appliances) primarily in the regional shopping centers and the CBD, but rarely in the smaller neighborhood shopping areas. This is the most general pattern for the metropolis.

In short, retailing in the metropolis tends to be distributed according to a hierarchical geographic pattern. At the bottom of the hierarchy are the neighborhood shopping centers. These draw customers primarily from the immediate zone around them. Of course, neighborhood shopping centers vary in size and their trading areas vary in size and shape. But the trading areas generally tend to be circular or oval in shape, with some overlapping from adjacent trading areas. Thus, one can think of the whole of the metropolis as being divided into a series of "cells" of retailing, each of roughly similar importance. Above this level in the hierarchy is another series of larger cells. These are the trading areas of the regional shopping centers. In the outer fringes of the metropolis, these are likely to be planned shopping centers, though not always so. In the inner parts of the metropolis, they are not so often planned centers, but they are always significantly larger than mere neighborhood shopping centers. Since the cells in this case are larger than those for neighborhood centers, there are of course fewer of them. Finally, there is the CBD, whose trading area extends over the entire metropolis and usually for a considerable distance beyond. The number and quality of goods and services it provides are directly related to the buying power of this trading area. When two metropolitan areas are close to each other it is sometimes possible for a suburban shopping center to grow beyond the normal regional shopping center level. It can do this if it can draw enough customers away from both CBDs to gain a level of business approaching that of a CBD.

In the technical language of geography, what I have been describing is known as a *Central Place System*. A *Central Place* is a point at which goods and services are concentrated because so concentrating them is more efficient than trying to provide them everywhere, as in an economy based entirely on self-sufficiency. The individual store or barber shop is the simplest Central Place. Clusters of stores, as in a neighborhood center or the CBD, are successively more complex Central Places. The concept of Central Place Systems is useful not only in discerning some logical order within the metropolis, but in other geographic settings as well. It is useful in examining the relationships between the metropolis as a whole and the cities, towns, and villages in its hinterland. In some respects, such communities relate to each other and the metropolis in analogous ways to those described here for neighborhoods, regional centers, and the CBD. Likewise, the sort of metropolis being described in this chapter, one with only about one million people, depends on larger Central Places such as New York for certain services such as stock exchanging. That is, Central Place Systems can be continental or global in scope, with many more levels in the hierarchy than the three levels noted in our hypothetical metropolis. These wider implications of Central Place Systems will be discussed again in subsequent chapters, particularly in Chapter 7. So certain specific terms are introduced here.

Three concepts are essential to the understanding of Central Place Systems: range, threshold, and hierarchy. A good or service provided at a Central Place will attract customers from a particular zone around it. This area or attractive zone is the *range* of that good or service. The range of lower order goods and services is small; the range of higher order goods and services is great. Since a given store usually provides a considerable variety of goods, the range of the store will be a combination of these several ranges. The range of a cluster of stores in a neighborhood will be the combined ranges of the stores. And so on.

The *threshold* of a Central Place is that minimum level of business that will enable it to meet expenses and stay in business. For example, although hardware stores vary in size, there is a minimum level for such stores, a level determined by fixed costs such as wages, maintaining a minimum supply of nuts and bolts, and so on. The threshold of a neighborhood drugstore is relatively low, whereas the threshold of a furniture store is higher, and of a department store higher still.

Ranges and thresholds are related to each other in a dynamic way. If the situation is a stable one, the range of each Central Place is great enough to meet threshold requirements and leave a normal profit margin. But if thresholds rise—perhaps because of an increase in wages paid clerks or because of an increase in the size of inventory required—while ranges remain constant, some Central Places will be eliminated and adjacent Central Places will expand their ranges accordingly. Or, if thresholds remain constant while the ranges increase, as through an improvement in transportation that allows customers to come from greater distances with no more effort than before, then the Central Place can make a much greater profit than formerly. However, if this profit margin is large and obvious, competitive Central Places may be established to tap this same potential. Then a new equilibrium will emerge and remain until ranges or thresholds again change.

The concept of *hierarchy* in Central Place Systems assumes that trading areas overlap in a stepwise fashion according to the level of the goods and services provided, from lower order ones to higher order ones. Thus, the range of a neighborhood center (or village, in a rural area) is both its own range for the services it provides, and simultaneously part of the range of a regional shopping center (or town or small city, in a rural area) for the higher order services that it cannot provide (because it is too small and has too many competitors). And so on, for the various levels of the hierarchy.

A hierarchy implies *dominance*. Thus, we can think of the different levels in a Central Place hierarchy as dominating the Central Places below them and within their range, and, in turn, being dominated by those Central Places above them, that is, within whose range they fall. Of course, another way of getting at hierarchy is in terms of degrees of accessibility or centrality. The chief center of a Central Place System has more centrality or accessibility than any other. The more populous a Central Place System and the larger the average income, the greater the number of steps it is possible to have in the hierarchy. The Central Place System of Metropolitan New York-northeastern New Jersey has more steps in the hierarchy than implied in our discussion of a hypothetical metropolis. The Central Place System of the United States has more steps still.

The Pattern of Services: Some Complexities

Of course, the geographic pattern of services is not quite as simple as such a discussion implies. Retailing itself varies from such a pattern in special cases to be noted later in this chapter. Further, retailing is only one of the services provided in a metropolis; other services follow Central Place principles in some ways, but in other ways they do not. Some of these variations on Central Place themes will now be noted.

Wholesaling is an interesting example. In many ways, the locational problem of the wholesaler is analogous to that of the retailer. He, too, has to select a location acceptable to his customers, but his customers are retailers and manufacturers rather than housewives. Whereas the retailer is much concerned with the geographic location of households and the income of those households (so that his range will include enough potential customers to meet his threshold), the wholesaler is concerned with the geographic location of stores and factories (so that his range will include enough potential customers to meet *his* threshold).

Obviously, the location of wholesaling is dynamically related to the location of retailing and manufacturing, just as the location of retailing is dynamically related to general population movements in the metropolis. However, the range of the retailer, even the specialty store in the CBD, often does not extend very far beyond the metropolis itself. But the wholesaler's range is normally greater; though a high percentage of his business may be within the metropolis itself, his range often extends for hundreds of miles beyond the metropolis. In other words, wholesaling is one of the higher order services.

In the metropolis of the late nineteenth and early twentieth centuries, wholesaling was usually highly concentrated in a cluster of wholesaling houses on the fringe of the CBD. Clustering was an advantage in attracting customers, just as clustering in retailing attracts customers. The great concentration of retailing in the adjacent CBD was an advantage, and from a central location other retailers could also be served. In those days, manufacturing also tended to concentrate in the inner portions of the metropolis, particularly in a zone surrounding the CBD. Railroads were the main transport link with places beyond the metropolis and the main rail terminals were usually near the CBD. Indeed, wholesaling was usually on the side of the CBD nearest the rail terminals.

But in recent decades, the locational matrix has shifted.

More of the retailing is on the fringes of the metropolis than before, in the new suburban shopping centers. Manufacturing is more widely dispersed in the metropolis, more often on the outer fringes of the metropolis than before. Railways and radial highways and limited access highways continue to make the general area of the CBD a point highly accessible to the whole metropolis, but at the same time circumferential highways and limited access highways make the fringes of the metropolis highly accessible, too. In addition, the widespread use of trucks tends to make the whole locational pattern more fluid than before. Because the routes that trucks can follow are so numerous there is greater freedom in locational choice than before. So we should not be surprised that although the old wholesaling districts near the CBD tend to persist, partly through inertia, wholesaling houses have also tended to disperse more widely, particularly to the fringes of the metropolis.

Though the customer tends to be a king in retailing and wholesaling locational choices, he is just a commoner or at best a lesser lord in relation to many other metropolitan services. Many of the services provided in the metropolis are monopolies or quasi-monopolies. Though most monopolists are concerned with pleasing their customers in terms of selecting desired locations, still, there is less opportunity for the customers to make their wishes directly known. Government, by law, has a monopoly in providing many services. Postal services are an example. In a very broad way, post office locations reflect Central Place principles. But they do not respond as readily to the advantages of hierarchical divisions in level of services. Nor do they respond as rapidly to changes in the locational mix of the metropolis, to changes in range based on transport innovations, to population shifts, and so on. Similarly, though welfare offices no doubt tend to be located somewhat according to Central Place patterns, the welfare clients are in a poor position to withdraw their business if the locations are in fact very inconvenient. Local government services, such as those associated with city hall, police, fire, and education, tend to be somewhat more responsive to Central

Place principles and to dynamic changes in the geography of the metropolis than are services provided by more distant governments. But even in this case, the "customers" often find it hard to make their collective wishes known to the proper officials.

Similarly, medical services are semi-monopolistic in nature. Entrance to the medical profession is controlled by the professionals, not the general public. Hospitals and other health centers are sometimes supported by taxation and sometimes by contributions. Generally, medical fees reflect the ability to pay, but there are also free services and subsidized services. Thus, it is not surprising that in some respects the distribution of medical services closely follows Central Place principles and in other respects it does not. The scattering of the offices of general practitioners through the metropolis is analogous to the distribution of neighborhood stores, the concentration of specialists often found in the CBD is analogous to the concentration of other higher order goods and services there, and the lesser clusterings of other specialists at various points in the metropolis is analogous to the regional shopping centers.

Yet in many American metropolitan areas there is a medical complex that does not fit these patterns. Such a complex includes several hospitals clustered close together, a university medical school, the offices of many specialists and medical technicians, stores selling medical equipment, testing laboratories, and so on. Such a complex *may* be located at a point that is highly accessible to the whole of the metropolis, but not necessarily. Such complexes have usually grown gradually from some initial node, such as a hospital or university medical school. They reflect the need of specialized professionals to be near each other for consultation and the like more than they reflect the need of the specialist to be accessible to those in need of medical care. In short, such complexes are an exception to Central Place patterns. They are examples of *specialized functional areas,* which will be discussed later. In general, one can assume that the more competitive a service is, the more likely it is to conform to Central

Place principles, including responsiveness to dynamic changes in the distribution of population or other distributions in the metropolis.

Even in essentially competitive situations, there are exceptions to what one might expect according to a Central Place interpretation. Such exceptions appear to have become more numerous in recent decades, perhaps indicating that Central Place patterns are of declining importance in the geography of the metropolis even though they are still the general rule. Such exceptions include (1) arterial commercial developments, (2) ribbon developments along highways, oriented to the flow of traffic *through* an area rather than to the population living in the area, and (3) specialized functional areas. By arterial commercial developments, I mean the tendency for furniture stores, appliance stores, discount houses, and the like to locate on the outer margins of the metropolis at nodal points along the arterial routes. Perhaps the great space requirements of stores of this type partially account for this. Such stores are also found according to what one would assume from Central Place ideas, but one cannot deny that more of them are found in nodal arterial sites than Central Place ideas would suggest.

By ribbon developments I mean the pattern of restaurants, drive-ins, service stations, motels, bars, and bargain stores locating in strings along major routes. Most of these types of establishments are also found at various other points in the metropolis, distributed according to Central Place notions. Restaurants, for example. Neighborhood shopping areas usually have several so-called greasy spoons; these are restaurants with low ranges and low thresholds. For the more attractive and more expensive restaurants, one generally has to look farther afield. Their distribution corresponds to the regional shopping centers. The most exclusive restaurants and the most specialized ones are often found in the CBD. This is the historic Central Place pattern. Yet one cannot deny that there has also been a strong affinity for ribbon locations in recent years.

Besides the medical complexes previously referred to, there are other examples of specialized functional areas: automobile sales areas, college and university complexes, governmental complexes, and business office complexes. In recent years, as retailing has somewhat declined in the CBD, the CBD has tended to become more and more a CGC, a Central Government Complex. Besides the many specifically governmental offices, there are also concentrations of tax consultants, lawyers, and other specialists in dealing with government. Often, the CBD is also a CBOC, a Central Business Office Complex. In addition to a clustering of the offices of major corporations, it may include a closely related cluster of accountants, tax consultants, lawyers, advertising specialists, public relations specialists, business associations, labor union offices, and so on.

Some Contemporary Changes in Service Geography

Almost ceaseless locational flux is the name of the game in a modern metropolis. There is nothing necessarily fixed or permanent about a particular system of locating services. As population distribution changes, so must the service pattern, insofar as it is directly responsive to the desires of consumers for locational convenience. Similarly, changes in income distribution may alter the system. For example, rising incomes may mean that middle- and upper-level goods and services are purchased more often than previously, whereas lower order goods may be purchased no more often than before. This could tend to cause the regional centers and the CBD to grow in relation to the neighborhood centers. Contrarily, falling incomes as in an economic depression could enhance the neighborhood centers in relation to the others. Likewise, if there is innovation in the technology or management associated with providing services, the geography of services must adjust accordingly. For example, increasing specialization and the use of very expensive equipment in medicine have tended to encourage concentration, as in medical complexes, and to reduce the importance of medical Central Place patterns. Of course, any change in transport technology will affect the pattern. For example, many of the deviations away from the

Central Place pattern noted in this chapter seem closely related to the coming of limited access highways.

Whether contemporary changes in the service geography of the metropolis are rapid or not depends on one's point of view. If the service geography of the metropolis of the late nineteenth and early twentieth centuries is assumed to be the norm, then the changes of recent decades have been very rapid and dramatic. But if we look at the *potentialities* in contemporary technology and in new ideas about how services might be organized, then the service geography of the contemporary metropolis is hopelessly archaic. No doubt the truth lies somewhere in between.

I do not want to suggest that the service geography of the metropolis must always change rapidly. Indeed, there are countervailing forces that tend to freeze, or stabilize, a particular locational pattern once it is established. The services themselves are major sources of employment. Since service workers may choose their residences with respect to the location of their employment and be loathe to change residences readily, the service pattern may tend to stabilize itself regardless of other changes in the metropolis. For example, a residential area attractive to doctors and near a medical complex will help to stabilize the location of that complex. Similarly, the mutual locational dependence between certain services and certain types of manufacturing may stabilize the locational pattern for both. For example, small-scale manufacturing by small firms often concentrates near the CBD because the small firm is often very dependent on the ability to hire services rather than providing them internally.

Further, the costs of moving deter a service establishment from changing location unless there are very clear advantages at some new site. Likewise, since habit is an important aspect of the consumer's locational choice, the service establishment risks losing customers by a move. Lastly, the manager of the service establishment has many things on his mind besides its location and relation to the surrounding environment, so he may be only dimly aware of locational changes going on around him. In short, there is inertia or resistance to locational change in the metropolis as well as pressures from many sources for movement. So locations change more slowly than they might otherwise. Perhaps this tendency to balance change with stability is important in helping metropolitans to keep their sanity.

Two changes now apparently occurring seem of particular importance. First, there appears to be a general tendency toward a "flattening" of the traditional Central Place System within the metropolis. Secondly, there appears to be a tendency toward more and more dispersal of the metropolis. By a flattening of the Central Place System, I mean a tendency for the regional shopping centers to grow in relation to either the neighborhood centers on the one hand or the CBD on the other. There appears to be a tendency for many older neighborhood shopping centers to decline or die out. Brian Berry has noted similar tendencies in the countryside and has aptly described this as a "selective thinning" of Central Places at the lower levels of the Central Place hierarchy. But in the rapidly developing suburban fringes of the metropolis this process might be more accurately described as the "selective aborting" of the lower levels of the hierarchy. That is, true neighborhood shopping areas (as opposed to regional shopping areas or ribbon developments) may simply fail to develop.

Concurrently, though the CBD is continuing to grow as a governmental center and business office center, it is not maintaining the lead it once had in many other services such as retailing. This is not to say that the CBD is not the dominant service center of the metropolis any more; it still is, and will continue to be for some time, perhaps always. But its growth has not been sufficient to maintain its former lead over competing points in the expanding Central Place System. The most effective competition for the CBD has not come from the bottom of the hierarchy, the neighborhoods; it has come from the in-betweens, the regional centers, the arterial nodes, the ribbon developments, and the specialized functional areas. Consequently, the whole Central Place System appears more flattened or squashed than before.

No doubt urban renewal efforts, often concentrated in or around the CBD, have retarded this process somewhat, but that they have actually arrested or reversed the process seems doubtful. The willingness of the public to thus concentrate urban renewal funds in the support of a particular service geography (apparently in the belief that they are saving the metropolis as a whole) seems rooted in habit and traditional mental maps about what the service geography of the metropolis is and ought to be. Such mental maps are subject to change as a more flattened pattern becomes, itself, traditional. Perhaps the metropolis of the future will be spending urban renewal funds to maintain a more flattened pattern against a reviving, sharply hierarchical, pattern.

By a tendency toward metropolitan dispersal, I mean more than the outward spread of sprawling suburbs, more even than the nature of the suburban areas themselves: regional shopping centers, specialized functional areas, arterial nodes, ribbon developments, new-found role of manufacturing areas as well as traditional role of dormitories and places to rear children. I mean also the expansion of the commuting area far beyond the built-up area of the metropolis to embrace whole zones or regions of countryside and their towns and villages. Alternative terms for metropolitan dispersal could be "erosion of the rural-metropolitan boundary" or "megalopolitanization."

The old, sharp distinctions between urban and rural were rooted in clear differences in accessibility in the two types of areas. But the cone of accessibility is flattening not only within the metropolis, but also between the metropolis and its immediate hinterland. Consequently, the outer margin of the metropolis in an economic and functional sense is indistinct. The service geography of the metropolis cannot help but be affected by this. The attractive power of the metropolis for commuting for employment or for services now extends fifty miles or more and this would appear to favor regional shopping centers, ribbon developments, arterial nodes, and specialized functional areas more than traditional Central Place patterns.

Whatever the service geography of the future metropolis (or megalopolis) will be, it will reflect conflicts among the competing desires of the inhabitants, particularly conflicts between the desire for nearness and other desires that can only be fulfilled through some measure of concentrating services. It will involve compromises, allowing the desire for nearness to be met in some cases (particularly with lower order goods and services) and other desires to be met in other cases (particularly with higher order goods and services). It will involve some situations in which the individual customer is truly king, or at least a crown prince; in those situations, the pattern will respond rapidly to wishes for transformation of the traditional geographic compromises. In other situations, geographic change will come more slowly because the individual will find more difficulty in making his wishes known to those in authority. The relative mix of service expenditures—that is, what proportion is supported through taxation and what proportion is spent by individuals—will have a great deal to do with this, as will what proportion of individual expenditures is used for routinized, standardized goods and services as opposed to highly specialized services such as medicine, higher education, and the like.

That the service geography of the future metropolis will differ from that of the present seems clear; locational flux is inherent in a metropolitan economy. But just how different it will in fact be is hard to say, because locational inertia and rigidity are also part of the metropolis.

CHAPTER 4

Manufacturing in the Metropolis

The regularities in the location of services discussed in the last chapter help to give geographic coherence and order to the metropolis. But what about manufacturing locations? Manufacturing is almost as important as services in the life of the metropolis, so the location of manufacturing is a very important part of the overall economic geography of such places. Can we assume that the same kind of hierarchical locational pattern that applies to services also applies to manufacturing? If not, is the pattern simply a random and incoherent one, unexplainable except in terms of the whims of individual manufacturers? Neither is true. There is a locational logic to the pattern, but, in most cases, it is somewhat different from what one would expect on the basis of Central Place theory or service geography in general.

Within the metropolis, manufacturing tends to be where the population wants it to be. But where do they want it be be? Insofar as the manufacturer is seeking a profit, he must consider the effects of alternative locations on profits. But the general public may not want manufacturing around at all. The traffic, noise, smoke, and smells associated in the public mind with manufacturing often make it undesirable, especially for residential areas. The public wants to reduce or eliminate such obtrusiveness. If this wish were fully granted, manufacturing might be excluded entirely from the metropolis or restricted to remote, nonresidential, suburban locations.

But the public has a contradictory set of wishes, too. It wants to be able to tax the manufacturer and wants the job opportunities provided by him. These job opportunities include those directly in the factory and also the service jobs that minister to the service needs of the factory and the factory workers.

So the general public has a big stake in the success of the manufacturer, and therefore must be concerned with allowing him to pick sites he considers potentially profitable. Most metropolitan populations are "hung up" to some degree on the horns of this dilemma of disliking the obtrusiveness of manufacturing close by and yet liking the taxes and jobs provided by successful locational choices in manufacturing. Therefore zoning laws that regulate manufacturing locations in most metropolitan areas are compromises, restricting the freedom of choice of the manufacturer to some degree and yet usually not deviating markedly from general locational patterns based on profitability. For a detailed understanding of the location of manufacturing within a *specific* metropolis, it is necessary to study the zoning map of that metropolis, but for a more general understanding this is not necessary. In the more general case, locational profitability is a better guide. However, zoning laws reflect *past* locational compromises and hence they are a significant inertial force in maintaining established locational patterns.

The manufacturer seeks a location from which he can make a profit. Some argue that he seeks the location from which he can maximize his profit, while others argue that he simply seeks the location from which he can get a level of profit that is satisfactory to him. In any case, a locational decision is usually a long-range decision. The costs of moving vary, from relatively low costs, much the same as for retailing, to many times higher, for those types of manufacturing that require heavy investment in highly specialized buildings and equipment, such as steelmaking or oil refining. The greater the cost of moving, the less frequently the manufacturer moves and the more long-range a given locational decision is.

All locational decisions are made not only in the context of the current geography of the metropolis, but also in the context of guesses about the future economic geography of the metropolis. Very often, the manufacturer simply does not have enough information about either the present or future geography of the metropolis to make optimum choices. However, it seems safe to assume that the poorer the choice turns out to be, the more likely he is to fail and thus be eliminated from the Manufacturing Map, or the more likely he is to move to a better location. Hence, it can be assumed that in a broad, general way the Manufacturing Map of the metropolis reflects the profitability of different locations.

To increase profits, one can either increase the demand for a product or decrease the costs of producing it, or both. However, to simplify the following discussion, it is assumed here that the manufacturer chooses locations primarily in order to reduce costs. It is assumed that he seeks a *least-cost location*. Costs are of two sorts, *site costs*, or those actually incurred at the manufacturing site itself, and *accessibility costs*, or the costs of moving people or things to and from the site. Examples of site costs include the land, the buildings, the machinery, upkeep, taxes, and basic wages. Examples of accessibility costs include commuting costs for workers, transport costs for assembling raw materials at the site and for transporting the finished product to customers, nearness to services such as gas lines, and nearness to centers of business news and gossip.

It is only as these vary geographically about the metropolis that they affect the locational choice. For example, if land taxes were the same everywhere, they would not affect the locational decision. But since they do vary geographically, particularly between downtown sites and more peripheral sites and among political jurisdictions (especially city versus suburb), land taxes do definitely affect the locational choices made.

Of course, it is the *totality* of costs at a site that is imporant, rather than each of these costs taken by itself. For example, a location might have low land costs, high taxes, low commuting costs, and high transport costs while another location has high land costs, low taxes, high commuting costs, and low transport costs. In such a case, the choice between the two would be made on the basis of the overall arithmetic, not any one factor.

Accessibility Costs

Accessibility costs include those related to raw materials, markets, labor, services, and information.

The costs of moving raw materials to the site from their sources within the metropolis are often high, particularly if the metropolis is large and congested. Indeed, it may cost as much to truck a raw material ten miles *across* a metropolis as it does to truck it a hundred miles *between* metropolitan areas or between a rural area and the metropolis. This is particularly important in relation to total costs when the raw material is of relatively low value in relation to its weight, when the finished product weighs much less than the raw material used, and when the industry is highly automated.

For example, petroleum refineries and traditional electrical generating plants are usually very close to piers, pipe lines, or rail junctions. For generating plants using atomic power, other considerations enter. Similarly, meat packing plants are usually near the stockyard terminals, and flour mills are near piers or rail terminals. The problem of reducing costs by locating near the source of raw materials is a relatively simple one when, as in the above cases, there is only one major source of raw materials. But suppose the manufacturing plant will be using a variety of raw materials from a variety of sources, from many different rail terminals, truck terminals, warehouses, and highway routes within the metropolis, what then? Then, it becomes a complex geometric problem, in which the manufacturer must choose his location by applying relative weights to the different directions from which the supplies might come. His choice will be some kind of compromise within a zone accessible to all.

The problem is further complicated when some or all of his raw material sources are local manufacturers rather than merely the major transport terminals. In a complex modern economy, the output of one factory often becomes the raw material of another. Indeed, the by-product of one factory or even the waste product of one factory may ultimately become the raw material of another. This dependence of various manufacturers on each other as sources of raw materials and markets for products is a major factor in producing industrial clustering. Sometimes, this clustering is pronounced enough to produce an *industrial complex* in a particular section of the metropolis. For example, a petroleum refinery may initially locate near a pipe line terminal. Subsequently, a petrochemical plant may be established nearby to further refine part of the output of the refinery. Still later, a plastics plant may be located adjacent to the petrochemical plant to use part of its output. Then, other manufacturers such as boat makers or furniture makers using plastics as major raw materials may locate nearby, too. Gradually, an industrial complex emerges through accretion. Thus, the need for accessibility to raw materials produces two kinds of clusterings, *general clusterings* related to major transport terminals such as waterfront locations or rail terminals, and more *specific industrial clusterings* related to the interdependence among the various plants themselves.

The significance of the location of *market outlets* depends very much on two questions: (1) the nature of the product (weight, size, perishability) and (2) the size of the market area served. If the product is more difficult and more expensive to transport and store than most of the raw materials going into it, then locating near the ultimate customers may be more important than locating near the sources of raw materials. For example, a custard stand making frozen custard from a dry mix has relatively nonperishable raw materials, but a highly perishable product. So, it locates near its market, perhaps a street corner frequented by teen-agers. A newspaper is another example. Newsprint is relatively nonperishable. But once a newspaper has been printed on it, the product is highly perishable. The demand for yesterday's newspaper is about equivalent to the demand for Christmas trees on December 26. So, a location in the center of the metropolis is chosen to make distribution quick and easy. Many types of manufacturing, particularly food processing, add large quantities of water to other ingredients. Since water is a ubiquitous raw material in the metropolis, and since water is heavy and expensive to transport after being made part of the product, it is often cheapest to locate centrally to the market served rather than in terms of other considerations. The location of breweries and soft drink bottling plants reflects this. Sometimes a product may actually weigh no more than the combined raw materials and yet the product may be more expensive to transport because it is so much bulkier, as in the case of assembled products. Thus, there are advantages in locating an assembly plant for office equipment in a place central to the market area served.

The sizes of the market areas served vary greatly and the significance of different locations varies accordingly. The market area of a custard stand or small bakery may be only a neighborhood or a district of the metropolis. For small establishments of this kind, locating in order to maximize demand is usually more important than least-cost considerations. The market area of a print shop may be essentially the metropolis as a whole. The market area of a metropolitan newspaper, large bakery, or brewery may be essentially the metropolis plus its hinterland. The market area of a detergent factory may be the nation. But the market area of a machine tool plant may be almost the entire world.

In short, some manufacturers are really manufacturer-retailers within part or all of the metropolis; other manufacturers may be manufacturer-retailers within the metropolis, but also sell through wholesalers and retailers beyond the metropolis; for still other manufacturers, sales within the metropolis itself are of minor importance in comparison with sales to distant areas. The more completely the manufacturer is a manufacturer-retailer for his home metropolis, the more completely the pattern of advantageous locations resembles that of the Central Place hierarchy. However, in the hypothetical metropolis being discussed here, one of only about one million population, only two steps in the hierarchy may be clearly evident, neighborhood concentrations and concentrations near the CBD. In very large metropolitan areas such as New York, the intermediate levels in the hierarchy may be more evident. For a manufacturer whose business is neatly divided between sales within the metropolis and outside it, a location near the CBD may provide easy access to the metropolitan market and also to more distant markets through the transport terminals located near the CBD. For the manufacturer oriented to distant markets, nearness to major transport lines and terminals is the only requirement. Thus, he is more free to locate near the periphery of the metropolis along rail spurs or the access points of limited access highways.

Locating with respect to the residences of particular worker groups, such as low-wage groups or groups with special skills, is probably less important than it once was in the manufacturing pattern of the metropolis. When most workers either walked to work or used public transportation services, it was essential to locate either near the homes of the workers or near a point where the public transportation system focused, such as near the CBD. Otherwise, one could not count on a steady labor supply. But insofar as the private automobile has superseded these forms of travel, almost any point in the metropolis can attract a sufficient labor supply. Even plants paying relatively low wages can often obtain enough workers though located in the suburbs. But plants employing cheap female labor, such as in the needle trades, still find it an advantage to cling to core locations.

At least part of the unemployment problem of slum areas today is caused by the flight of industry from core areas that are near the slums and accessible by public transportation; hence, recent efforts by governmental bodies to attract factories back to the core or to provide public transportation directly to outlying plants. However, efforts to attract industry back to the core are unlikely to be very successful unless the combined advantages of a core location—including the effects of all locational factors discussed in this chapter plus a governmental subsidy—are greater than those of a peripheral location.

In certain cases, there are advantages in locating with reference to the residences of particular employee groups with special skills or educational backgrounds. For example, in large metropolitan areas such as New York, there are advantages to publishers in locating in the suburbs near large pools of well-educated middle class housewives. Similarly, highly specialized forms of manufacturing that employ large numbers of engineers find it easier to attract such engineers if located in suburban areas. Thus, while the core has some remaining pull because of accessibility to low-wage labor there is also a contrary pull to the suburbs because of accessibility to highly skilled labor groups. In general, though, the location of labor supplies does not strongly affect the manufacturing pattern within the contemporary metropolis.

The metropolis has a greater variety of services than nonmetropolitan areas. These include both utilities (telephone, electricity, gas, frequent mail delivery, water, sewer, and waste disposal) and a wide variety of other services (warehousing, wholesaling, accounting, billing, employment services, tax experts, and consultants of all types). Some of these services are provided by governments and others by private firms. The attraction of such services is a major factor in favoring metropolitan manufacturing locations over nonmetropolitan locations.

But do the locations of such services affect the distribution of manufacturing within the metropolis itself? In general, such services are accessible enough from all points in the metropolis so that they do not have much effect on the choice of a specific location. However, such services are somewhat more accessible from the core than peripheral locations. Therefore, core locations are particularly advantageous for small firms. The larger the firms, the more they are able to either provide such services themselves or attract these services to them whatever location they may choose. For small firms, there are great advantages in clustering together in the core where the total volume of demand for such services is enough to warrant their organic development. The core of the metropolis has long been the preeminent seedbed for plants by new firms. By locating in the core where there is usually manufacturing space for rent and where there is the greatest variety of business services-for-hire, the new firm can minimize its capital outlay. If the firm grows and prospers, it gains a greater freedom in choosing a manufacturing location within the metropolis. But as a greater and greater proportion of all manufacturing is concentrated in large firms, this historic role of the core as a seedbed for new enterprises is correspondingly reduced.

We should avoid the temptation of assuming that all accessibility costs are easily computed in dollars and cents, a simple arithmetic, algebraic, or geometric problem for the manufacturer. One of the historically most important of all accessibility costs is that of obtaining accurate and up-to-date business news. Since business gossip is neither shipped by the ton nor separately charged for on telephone bills, we cannot readily compute the cost of such accessibility. Yet in those types of manufacturing subject to frequent changes in style, such as women's dresses, ready and continuing access to business news is essential to staying in business. Face-to-face contact, as at businessmen's clubs, bars, and restaurants, is often crucial for the spread of such business gossip. The need for such contact favors both the clustering of certain types of manufacturing close together—as in the case of the garment district of New York—and the more diffused clustering of many types of manufacturing in the core.

It is true that the great variety of information services available to the contemporary manufacturer (besides such services as the telephone and the mail, there are many more specialized ones such as messenger services, specialized news services, various trade journals, and so on) at almost any location in the metropolis has reduced the need for face-to-face contact. The videophone and other incipient advances in communications may reduce this need still further. But the need for face-to-face contact persists. It is least significant in those forms of manufacturing that are highly routinized and standardized, such as most mass production. It is most significant in those forms of manufacturing that are unstandardized, subject to frequent changes in demand, and organized primarily in small plants.

Site Costs

The major site costs, or costs actually incurred at the site of the manufacturing plant itself, are wages, the cost of buildings and machinery, land, and taxes. Wages are often a major cost to the manufacturer, but for a given type of work they do not usually vary enough within a specific metropolis to affect manufacturing locations significantly. In very large metropolitan areas there may be slightly lower wage rates at the periphery than at the core, but in most metropolitan areas the wage rates are relatively standard throughout. Wage differentials were once somewhat more significant, but this was before the locational fluidity introduced by the automobile and before widespread standardization of wage rates through unionization. Similarly, the cost of buildings and machinery and their maintenance may vary somewhat in different parts of the metropolis, but usually such differences are too small to affect the Manufacturing Map greatly.

The other two site costs, land and taxes, are often very important in the locational choices of manufacturers. The market price for metropolitan land is closely related to its accessibility. This price is based on competition among the potential users of a given site. The most central part of the metropolis, the CBD, has accessibility advantages for nearly all urban land uses: retailing, governmental functions, office work, manufacturing, and so on. But since centrality is even more important for services such as retailing than for most forms of manufacturing, such services can afford to pay a higher price for land than manufacturing can. Hence, though manufacturing often clusters in a zone peripheral to the CBD, the CBD itself usually has little manufacturing, but many services. Similarly, centrality is usually more crucial in manufacturing than in residential location. Therefore, manufacturers can usually afford to outbid residential land users unless great scenic, sentimental, or historic value is attached to a specific site. In short, we can conceive of a hypothetical metropolis in which land values are highest at the center and gradually diminish in all directions, becoming lowest at the periphery of the metropolis.

In such a simplified situation, where the manufacturer would actually locate between the center and the periphery would be based on a balance between the importance of the various accessibility costs to him in his particular type of manufacturing and the price of the land, which would reflect the advantage of accessibility to others as well as himself. For a printer and publisher of a metropolitan newspaper the advantages to be found in reducing accessibility costs in transporting newsprint (from nearby waterfronts or rail terminals), in distributing the newspaper daily, in being near advertising agencies, and in assembling the news might more than offset the very high market price for centrally accessible land in or near the CBD.

But for a branch auto-assembly plant receiving its parts primarily from sources outside the metropolis, selling its product partly within the metropolis but also in a large region beyond it, providing many of its own services through its own large organization, and having relatively little need for business gossip because it follows production orders from company headquarters in another city, a location at the very fringes of the metropolis might be a cheaper and more rational choice. The lower price of the land might easily offset the loss in accessibility to the center of the metropolis, particularly if the site were near a rail spur or limited access highway and provided with all metropolitan utilities.

The choices of other manufacturers would lie on the continuum between these two extremes, varying with the details in each case. Of course, the market price of land is not in fact a simple cone, highest at the center and diminishing equally in all directions. There are lesser peaks in land prices at other points beyond the CBD, such as at major highway junctions. So the effects of land prices on manufacturing location are actually very complex.

Taxes affect manufacturing location primarily through the real estate tax, the primary tax base of most metropolitan areas in the United States. Real estate taxes tend to reflect the profitability of a site and hence tend to reflect accessibility, though this is modified by the condition of the buildings or machinery at the site. There are usually marked differences in real estate taxes in various parts of the central city of the metropolis, with the highest being in the CBD. Often there are wide variations in real estate taxes among different suburbs as well as between the central city and the suburbs. Other forms of taxation generally affect the location of manufacturing less markedly, primarily because the taxes are uniform over wide geographic areas rather than varying from one parcel of real estate to another. For example, if the central city imposes an income tax or sales tax while the suburbs do not, this may encourage manufacturing to move to the suburbs, but it will not particularly affect location within the central city itself. One would have to pay the same tax no matter where one located in the central city, so such taxes would not affect choices among sites within the central city.

Hence the location of manufacturing in the metropolis largely reduces to the question of accessibility—to a balancing of the relative needs for accessibility in various forms of manufacturing and the relative costs of accessibility, that is, land prices and taxes (especially real estate taxes). The manufacturer is always caught on the horns of this locational dilemma. If his initial choice is satisfactory, it remains satisfactory only so long as the balance between the two remains much the same. If the balance shifts radically so that a new location would be much more desirable, he will still hesitate to move until the anticipated benefits of the new location definitely exceed the costs of moving. Hence the Manufacturing Map of the metropolis usually changes only slowly and gradually unless other aspects of the geography of the metropolis change rapidly and radically.

Manufacturing Districts

Although the dilemma of locational choice is different for each manufacturer, there are enough similarities in the choices made so that well-defined manufacturing districts contain most of the manufacturing of the metropolis. Such clustering is induced by similar dependencies such as: (1) the general pattern of accessibility in the metropolis, (2) accessibility based on interlinkages among related manufacturers, as in a petrochemical industrial complex, or (3) political constraints, as in the case of zoning regulations. The more significant districts include (1) the CBD fringe, (2) waterfront and railroad concentrations, (3) concentrations on metropolitan highway radials, and (4) suburban clusters.

The CBD fringe contains a potpourri of industries, ranging from some of the oldest plants in the metropolis to some of the youngest. Some of the older plants remain in the CBD fringe because accessibility to the CBD or to the metropolis as a whole is still highly important. But many of the older plants remain in this zone simply through inertia, either because the costs of moving exceed the advantages of alternative sites or because the firm is not very alert to alternatives. The newer plants in the fringe are likely to be small ones, started "on a shoestring" and for which the shelter of the core is very attractive. Many, and perhaps most, of the plants, whether old or new, are those (1) needing raw materials from downtown rail terminals and warehouses or widely scattered sources in the metropolis, or (2) marketing in the inner core of the metropolis or the whole metropolis, or (3) relying on the low-wage labor of adjacent slums, or (4) depending heavily on hired services, or (5) needing face-to-face contacts in obtaining business news, or (6) combinations of these needs. Though the CBD fringe usually contains some large plants, the average size of the plant is usually less than for the metropolis as a whole. Though there may be some relatively new buildings, most of the manufacturing buildings are old and often relatively inefficient in terms of modern manufacturing techniques.

Most metropolitan areas are located on rivers, lakes, or oceans. Hence most of them have one or more waterfront districts. Most older metropolitan areas also have concentrations along the major rail lines, including not only those near the major terminals, but also those strung along the rail lines and thus extending as belts through the metropolis. Generally, these manufacturing districts are dominated by industries consuming large quantities of bulk raw materials and/or shipping relatively heavy items to markets outside the metropolis, particularly to national markets. Thus, they are usually the so-called heavy industries. Often, they are much automated, so that nearness to labor supply is not a major consideration in location. Often, the plants are owned by major national corporations, which supply them with many of the business services and business information for which others must depend on nearness to the CBD. However, the pattern is complicated by the age of most such districts. There are often remnants in them of firms held there more by inertia than by major contemporary advantages of such a location. Similarly, the pattern is often confused because the older districts of this type often border on the CBD fringe. The boundary between such rail and waterfront districts and the CBD fringe is not always sharp.

There are usually clusters of manufacturing firms along some, though not all, of the major highway radials linking the CBD to the rest of the metropolis. Such clusters represent choices made along the continuum between high land cost and great accessibility near the center, and low land cost and low accessibility at the periphery. They also represent attraction to the ridge of high accessibility that extends outward from the CBD along these radial routes. In many respects, such linear clustering along metropolitan radial routes is analogous to similar developments in the location of services. Indeed, there is often much intermixing of manufacturing and retailing along such routes, particularly in the older portions nearest the CBD. Again, in the older parts, there is usually some evidence of inertia in plant location.

Suburban clusters are more nodal in character and are usually oriented to either circumferential highways or to the more recently developed limited access highways. Their nodal character is evident in their clustering near the access points of the limited access highways, in the very large size of many of these plants, and in the grouping of small or moderate sized plants in planned clusters, the industrial parks. Though these areas often have rail service, they are particularly oriented to truck transportation. Usually, their major markets lie beyond the metropolis in the nation as a whole or in major subdivisions of the nation, though if the metropolis is a large one it too may be a significant market. Their labor supply comes primarily from the suburbs and the peripheral zones of the central city, but also from a commuting zone extending beyond the metropolis for as much as fifty miles or more; their employment outreach greatly exceeds their in-reach, so that relatively few slum dwellers are employed in such plants.

Distance from the services of the CBD is a disadvantage, but not as much as one might expect since these plants are usually owned by major national corporations that can supply many such services internally. For the same reason, distance from the centers of business news in the CBD is less disadvantageous than for the small firm. Land is usually cheaper than in more central locations and real estate taxes are often lower. Buildings and equipment are new and oriented to contemporary manufacturing practice, particularly in terms of horizontal manufacturing lines rather than vertical manufacturing lines. Hence these districts have many advantages over the older manufacturing districts and one can anticipate their continued growth. As the network of limited access highways grows and accessibility is thus extended into the hinterland of the metropolis, the dispersal of manufacturing outward from the metropolis will be encouraged. Ultimately, most mass-production manufacturing may abandon most of the older districts in favor of such suburban nodes.

Summary and Conclusions

Constant flux in the location of manufacturing is just as common as it is for services. And perhaps even more so, because a manufacturer selling to national markets does not have to consider customer loyalty to a particular site as much as the retailer does. Yet there are inertial forces too, particularly the heavy fixed investment in particular types of manufacturing buildings and in machinery that may be very expensive to move. The major contemporary changes in the Manufacturing Map of the metropolis seem to parallel those in services. Thus, the accessibility cone is tending to flatten and manufacturing districts near the CBD are growing less rapidly than new nodal districts in the suburbs. Similarly, there is a general tendency toward metropolitan dispersal: for commuting to extend far beyond the borders of the metropolis and for new manufacturing nodes to emerge along the limited access highways beyond the metropolis itself. Likewise, the scattering of manufacturing along radial and circumferential highways parallels ribbon developments in retailing. And the growth of industrial complexes parallels the growth of service complexes.

Insofar as the Manufacturing Map parallels that of services it is due to similar accessibility needs. Insofar as the map is different, it is due to the greater orientation of manufacturing to areas beyond the metropolis (to external sources of raw materials and to regional or national markets), to a wider range of skills and wage levels, to a greater dependence on services external to the firm, to a greater need for space (land), to a greater variation in taxation patterns, and to somewhat more restrictive zoning.

CHAPTER 5

Primary Production in the Metropolis and Environs

Preceding chapters have demonstrated that, despite the apparent disorder of the metropolis, considerable regularity and predictability in the locational patterns of services and manufacturing are evident. But what about *primary* production: agriculture, forestry, mining, and the like? Is there any consistency in the locational patterns of these on the metropolitan periphery? This may seem like a silly question because it is traditional to think of the city (and hence the metropolis) as something quite distinct from, apart from, things of the land such as agriculture. It has been traditional to think of farmers as a different breed of men from metropolitans, more traditional, more family-oriented, and more oriented to communing with the sun and the wind and the soil. In America at least, this view of farmers as being so different was always partly mythological, based more on European traditions (including especially the sharp social stratification of Europe) than on actual observations of the American scene. But it was in part true in the past, particularly because of the greater isolation of rural areas.

However, the concept of metropolitan dispersal, discussed in previous chapters, has great meaning for primary production as well as for manufacturing and services. The nature of primary production cannot help being different when direct metropolitan influences extend for about fifty miles around the average metropolis and for greater distances around major metropolitan areas such as New York or Chicago. Fifty-mile circles around the metropolitan areas of the more populous parts of the United States (the East, the Great Lakes Littoral, the Gulf, and the Far West) include a significant proportion of the potential acreage available for primary production. Even in the less populated parts of the United States, such as the Great Plains or the Mountain West, a high proportion of the population lives in metropolitan areas. A map of the United States with fifty-mile circles around every metropolitan area is an impressive thing to see. Try it. It is particularly instructive in terms of how we should begin to think about primary production now and in the future. A significant proportion of our primary production now occurs in such a metropolitan context; therefore, locational patterns of primary production cannot be understood unless metropolitan locational forces are taken into account as well as the more traditional locational forces associated with such production.

Another aspect of the question is also important. Understanding the nature of land use on the periphery of the metropolis is important in anticipating future locational patterns of the metropolis itself. The primary production areas just beyond the built-up area of the metropolis provide the space into which the metropolis expands as it grows in population and appetite for land. Therefore, the primary production patterns of today are antecedent locational patterns of the metropolitan stores, factories, and residential areas of tomorrow. Today's pasture becomes tomorrow's suburban shopping center; today's gravel pit becomes tomorrow's unsightly, unsanitary, and unauthorized community dump in the midst of split levels. Today's strip mining area becomes tomorrow's attractive park or tomorrow's eyesore, depending on the circumstances. Today's cluster of Negro shanties on a portion of the "Old Plantation" becomes a huge and sprawling ghetto tomorrow, or, more hopefully, the nucleus of an area of integrated living. Locational patterns on the metropolitan margins often shape the details of the emerging metropolitan geography though they seldom determine all aspects of that geography.

Then, what are the locational patterns of primary production on the margins of our hypothetical metropolis? To avoid

78 / A PRIMER ON ECONOMIC GEOGRAPHY

excessive complications, it will be necessary to add two further characteristics to those already listed for our hypothetical metropolis in Chapter 3. First, let us assume that the hypothetical metropolis is located in the United States. There are great national variations in the nature of primary production, variations produced by general cultural differences, differences in traditional ways of organizing farming, differences in governmental regulation, subsidization, taxation of primary production, and so on. Secondly, let us assume that the geological and biological conditions in the fifty-mile zone are such as to permit a wide variety of crops and animals to be raised and a wide variety of minerals (particularly sand, gravel, clay, and stone) to be mined. Thus, our hypothetical metropolis could *not* be located in the most extreme northern parts of the country, in the arid Southwest, or in the midst of mountains such as the Appalachians or the Rockies. The locational forces discussed in this chapter would apply in those areas, too, but complicated by such extreme local conditions that their force would be much diminished and disguised.

Driving around the margins of our hypothetical metropolis, one would observe some apparently contradictory conditions. The scene would appear quite confusing: a mixture of flourishing farms; empty wasteland; gravel pits and quarries, some abandoned and some in use; scattered residential developments, some in nodes and some strung along the highways lacing the area; golf courses; woodland; greenhouses; wheat fields; scattered factories and warehouses and shopping centers; motels; private fishing lakes; abandoned farm buildings; very well-kept farm buildings; and so on. And on, mile after mile. Nor would all of these land uses be neatly sorted out into zones or distinctive areas. Instead, the pattern would appear rather disorderly, with the most unlikely land uses often found side by side. Why, for example, should a flourishing farm be surrounded by wasteland? Or a major quarry, with much attendant noise, dirt, and traffic, be set in the midst of a residential zone? Nowhere does the metropolis appear more disorderly, more confusing, than on its margins.

But the land use confusion on the borders of the metropolis is in fact more apparent than real. The patterns begin to make more sense, to seem more orderly and lawful, if we assume that they are primarily a product of forces relating to the metropolis itself and that the metropolis both *attracts* and *repels* primary production. Attraction is based in part on savings in transport costs; the metropolis is a major consumer of primary products and the producer can save on transporting costs by locating as close to this market as possible. In addition, the metropolis attracts because it represents things highly valued in our society: jobs for the farmer's wife or children (in services or manufacturing), access to college-prep schooling for the farmer's children, and access in general to the more varied and more specialized services available in the metropolis and its margins. It isn't just the bright lights that attract; a modern farm family wants top quality medical care and shopping opportunities just as much as any other family.

But the metropolis also *repels* primary production. Other land uses such as recreation, services, manufacturing, residences, transportation, and speculation compete with primary production for the land. Taxation, zoning, and other land-use regulation may also drive out the primary producer.

Hence the borders of the metropolis are a zone of transition, a zone of tension and conflict, in which the ever changing forces of attraction and repulsion war with each other for dominance. In the long run, the forces of repulsion tend to win out, but at any given time there is much waxing and waning of the strength of the opposing forces. In the United States, the land is primarily owned by individuals and this ownership is very widely dispersed. In an economically fluid situation such as I have been describing, it is not surprising that different owners perceive opportunity differently. As the metropolis encroaches, one farmer decides to hang on. But to pay his rising taxes, he has to intensify his farming, to derive some economic benefit from the encroachment. However, his neighbor decides to leave his land idle, waiting for speculative profits. Another neighbor sells right away to the first bidder, a casket manufacturer, and buys other farmland farther away from the metropolis. Another neighbor sells to a speculator who is fooled because the discount house he was anticipating as a customer decides to locate on cheaper land farther down the highway; the speculator decides to raise wheat until such time as he can sell the land at a profit. Confusion is to be expected when the indicators of the strength of the attracting and repelling forces are untrustworthy at times. A more detailed discussion of the nature of the attracting and repelling forces is now in order.

The Attracting Forces

As discussed previously, the primary producer may be attracted to the metropolis as a consumer of the great variety of things it has to offer as well as in the role of a producer selling to the metropolitan markets. But for simplicity's sake, this discussion will concentrate on his attraction as a producer. For further simplification, this discussion will include only agriculture and mining, ignoring other forms of primary production.

The best known theory of the location of agriculture in relation to costs of transporting goods to market is that initially developed by von Thunen, a nineteenth century economist and economic geographer. A modified version of that theory will be used here to clarify two aspects of agricultural attraction toward the metropolis: *intensification* and *zonation*. Wider applications of these ideas will be taken up in Chapter 9.

For the purposes of clarifying the role of transport costs, let us make a series of hypothetical assumptions about the metropolitan borderland: (1) it is a smooth plain, with no significant terrain barriers, and uniformity of soil fertility, (2) there are no non-agricultural land uses in the area (that is, no mining, quarrying, forestry, recreation, manufacturing, or other such land uses to distort the agricultural pattern), (3) the farmers are equal in abilities, education, access to capital, and so on, (4) there is a free market for farm products (that is, there are no acreage controls, subsidies, or other forms of governmental regulation), (5) the metropolis is the sole mar-

Primary Production in the Metropolis and Environs / 81

ket for the farm production (that is, none of the farmers sell to other metropolitan areas, other parts of the country, or other countries) and (6) none of the repelling forces discussed previously are operative. By making such gross and patently unrealistic assumptions it is possible to clarify the major factor we are concerned with here: the locational role of transport costs. After having read the following discussion, the reader may refer back to these assumptions and from them see how the actual situation might be a bit more complicated in the real world.

In such a situation, agriculture would tend to be most intensive at the margin of the built-up area of the metropolis and gradually decrease in intensity (become more extensive) away from the metropolis. By being intensive, I mean that the investment in buildings, machinery, and labor would tend to be high in relation to the investment in the land itself. Usually, this would mean relatively small acreage farms. By being extensive, I mean that the per-acre investment in buildings, machinery, and labor would be less. Usually, this would mean larger acreage farms. Why would intensity be greatest on the margins of the metropolis and decrease outward? Because the farmers located closest to the metropolis would have a distinct advantage over the others: their costs of transporting products to market would be lower. However, this advantage of centrality or nearness to market would not go unnoticed. It would soon come to be reflected in the price of the land.

So a kind of locational balance would emerge gradually. The farmer nearest the metropolis would have the lowest transport costs, but he would also have the highest price to pay for land; the farmer at a more distant site, say forty miles farther out, would have greater transport costs, but he would not have to pay so much per acre for his land. The farmer nearest the metropolis could resolve this dilemma by buying a smaller farm and investing more in it, in terms of buildings, machinery, or labor. This option would also be open to the farmer farther out, but there would not be as much incentive to do it since the per-acre price of the land in that area would be less. In short, the accessibility cone within the metropolis discussed in Chapter 4 in relation to factory sites also has effects on the intensity of agriculture at the margins of the metropolis.

Similarly, in our hypothetical situation, some types of farming would be attracted more strongly toward the metropolis than others. Transport costs vary from product to product. Products readily shipped in bulk, such as wheat, cost less to transport per mile than products less easily transported in bulk, such as eggs, milk, fruits, and vegetables. Perishability is also a factor. Ripe field corn is relatively nonperishable; fresh corn on the cob is highly perishable. And so on. Producers of perishables would be very much concerned with the *time* required to get to market as well as the actual per-mile cost. Therefore, there would tend to be a zonation of production. Farmers producing milk, eggs, decorative plants, fruits, vegetables, turf, and the like would derive the greatest advantage from a location close to the metropolis and would tend to locate in an inner ring just beyond the metropolis. Producers of other farm items, such as meat or grains, would derive less benefit from centrality, so they would tend to locate in a ring or rings farther out.

Such a hypothetical explanation would be of little value if it did not help in explaining contemporary patterns. The more populous a metropolitan area (and therefore the greater attraction of its markets), the more readily such patterns can be seen in its periphery. Because it is located between New York and Philadelphia, New Jersey is a good example of such tendencies. On the whole, the soils, climate, and terrain of New Jersey are not notably favorable to agriculture, though central New Jersey is somewhat advantageous. Many parts of the Middle West, Far West, and South have more favorable soils, climate, and terrain. But New Jersey's agriculture makes up for this by its location near New York and Philadelphia. Most of New Jersey is within fifty miles of either metropolis. It is not for nothing that New Jersey is known as the "Garden State"; but it is also an important producer of eggs, milk, and similar products. In *acreage* New Jersey is not an important farm state; but in *value* of production it is an important producer, particularly *value added* (milk or eggs produced from feedstuffs raised in other states more distant from metropolitan markets). No other whole state is quite such a vivid example of the attractive power of metropolitan markets, but the same phenomenon can be observed on a lesser scale around most of the larger metropolitan areas of the United States, certainly any with a population of one million or more.

True, nearness to the metropolis is not as advantageous for agriculture now as it was a few decades ago. Improvements in transportation and other factors discussed in greater detail in Chapter 9 enable areas hundreds of miles away to compete with nearby producers of fruits, vegetables, and the like. Further changes in transportation and in other factors can be anticipated. One might assume from this that the attractive power of the metropolis for agriculture at its periphery would one day vanish entirely. Perhaps it will. Yet the metropolis continues to generate new agricultural demands at the same time that it is generating innovations in transportation and the like. Sod farming is a good example, even though relatively small numbers of farmers in the periphery are involved in it. Sod farming is the growing of turf with which to make "instant lawns" around new housing developments or new schools, factories, or shopping areas. Essentially, it seems to be a product of affluence in the metropolis. A generation ago, most people were willing to just plant grass seed and wait. Similarly, the rise of "estate farming" at the periphery in recent years provides a new agricultural role for the periphery. The metropolitan owners, who want to combine farming with recreation and tax advantages, are attracted to locations in the metropolitan periphery more often than they are to more distant sites. To what extent such new forms of farming, originating in new agricultural demands by the metropolis, will offset less favorable developments is difficult to foresee.

Other forms of primary production, most particularly mining and quarrying, are also attracted toward the margins of the metropolis. Some of this is residual or inertial in nature. For example, the metropolis may have grown from an original nucleus of settlement on or around a mineral deposit. This was very often the case in the nineteenth century; hence, many of our metropolitan areas today had their historical origins in mining settlements. However, metropolitan areas today, and especially relatively new metropolitan areas today, seldom owe their primary raison d'être to mining. Economies-of-scale in transportation and mining tend to preclude the residential concentrations of large numbers of workers near mining sites. The nineteenth century case is an example of the metropolis moving to the mining rather than an example of mining moving to the metropolis. However, if a metropolis *is* found within a mining zone, the nearness of that metropolis and its markets may have residual effects on local mining. For example, coal mining in the northern Appalachians is probably buoyed to some extent by the transport savings involved in the nearness of many metropolitan areas. Put differently, transport advantages have helped coal to compete with more distant sources of power (such as petroleum, natural gas, or hydroelectric power) when the coal deposit is found in the periphery of a metropolis.

But such are special cases. The more general case involves the quarrying of stone, gravel, sand, and clay in the periphery of the metropolis. The *demand* for such products is related primarily to manufacturing and to new construction of buildings and highways. Hence this demand is highly concentrated today—primarily in metropolitan areas and especially on their suburban fringes. Such products are of relatively low value in relation to their weight; hence transport cost is usually a significant proportion of the total delivered cost. There are great transport advantages in producing them close to market. There is generally some production of them in the periphery of nearly every metropolis, despite variations in the natural occurrence of such minerals. Relatively low quality deposits may be mined close by in preference to higher quality deposits farther away unless the high quality, distant deposits have some unusual advantage (such as a cheap water route to the metropolis). The significance of such quarrying and mining on the fringes of the metropolis tends to be masked by the tendency to concentrate discussions of mining on the more glamorous kinds of mining: gold, uranium, petroleum, iron, and so on. But if either employment in mining or the dollar value of mining production is the clue to relative importance, then the mining of stone, sand, gravel, and clay is a major branch of the mining industry. A very high proportion of all mining of such materials occurs within fifty mile zones around the metropolitan areas.

Such a concentration of mining and quarrying presents a geographic dilemma. In the *short range,* such a concentration is clearly advantageous; it enhances the growth of the metropolis by providing relatively cheap raw materials for manufacturing and construction. But in the *long range,* there may be disadvantages. The metropolitan periphery is the zone into which the metropolis expands. Many kinds of mining and quarrying leave the land in conditions inappropriate for other forms of land use, such as residential development. Some day, land-use zoning may effectively limit the kinds of mining and quarrying permissible in the metropolitan periphery or ban all kinds; but, if so, metropolitans would have to be willing to pay the consequent higher costs for raw materials. If the metropolis continues to grow more affluent, it may be willing to do just that. Or, alternatively, metropolitan economies may invest more in research to produce innovations in mining or transportation that would resolve the dilemma. In short, the contemporary attraction of certain forms of mining and quarrying to the metropolitan periphery may or may not diminish in the future.

The Repelling Forces

But the metropolis repels primary production as well as attracting it. Wage rates are a factor, particularly in the case of agriculture. In the metropolitan periphery, the farmer has to compete with manufacturing and services for workers whereas the more distant farmer may be competing only with other farmers for labor. Consequently, agricultural wage rates often decline away from metropolitan areas. Other repelling factors include the higher tax rates associated with metropolitan areas and the tendency for metropolitan land-use zoning to discourage primary production.

But the most important single repelling force is the apparently insatiable demand of the modern metropolis for land in its periphery: land for diffusing clusters and ribbons of services, manufacturing, and residences; land for transportation; land for recreation; land for a variety of other purposes such as water supply, military protection, and so on; and land held for speculation on the assumption that the metropolis will continue to grow and continue to accelerate its demand for space in its periphery. Hypothetically, some of these land uses can be effectively combined with agricultural land use in multiple land-use systems. And some multiple land use does occur. For example, the fruit farmer who allows his customers the option of "picking their own" is combining farming and recreation. Or, part-time farmers who hold jobs in the metropolis may get more recreation from their farm than they do direct supplementary income. Or, the farmer may speculate while continuing farming. And so on. However, the general effect of these forces is to repel primary production away from the metropolis.

A major conclusion in Chapters 3 and 4 was that the metropolis is tending to become less tightly integrated than before, that it is tending to diffuse or disperse into the countryside surrounding it. The repelling effect of this dispersal on agriculture is least when it is nodal, in the form of relatively large clusters. It is greatest when it is of the ribbon type, paralleling the road network lacing the periphery. For it is precisely this kind of location that is of most value to the commercial farmer attracted to the metropolitan periphery by its large market potential. A peripheral location off the main roads might have less actual transport advantage than a site beyond the fifty mile zone but located on a good highway. Consequently, metropolitan ribbon development in the periphery is often accompanied by the growth of brush and other evidence of agricultural disuse on land without direct highway access.

Metropolitan populations are more affluent than any ever known before in history. They express part of their affluence in accelerating demand for land for outdoor recreation, particularly in the metropolitan periphery. Metropolitan recreational space demand associated with vacation periods of two

Primary Production in the Metropolis and Environs / 87

weeks or more is not necessarily expressed in the metropolitan periphery. But recreational demand through the rest of the year is strongly expressed in the area within convenient driving distance, particularly within the fifty mile zone around the metropolis. As a result, the metropolis is increasingly ringed by estates, golf courses, hunting camps, marinas, parks, children's camps, resorts, and the like. Generally, expansion of recreational land use is associated with the expansion of woodland.

Transportation and communication are essential to the metropolis, for the essence of the metropolitan economy is fluidity and movement. Of course, this characteristic of the metropolis is expressed most fully in the heart of the metropolis, in the CBD. There, the use of land for various aspects of transportation usually exceeds any other single land use. But this need to use land for transportation is felt throughout the metropolis and its periphery, and includes the necessity of providing links to the hinterland and other metropolitan areas. The need is greatest at the center and gradually declines in all directions. The great consumption of land in the periphery in recent years for limited access highways and airports has emphasized this point, but these are only the more obvious aspects of the general pattern.

In addition to metropolitan dispersal, recreation, and transportation, the metropolis makes many other space demands on its periphery, too many demands to readily classify: water supply areas, military camps, cemeteries, waste disposal areas, and so on.

Land speculation is a major factor. Since the metropolis has been expanding for a long time, one does not have to be particularly acute in business to realize that profits can be made from buying peripheral land and holding it for an anticipated rise in price. Nearly everyone owning land in the periphery is a land speculator to some degree, consciously or unconsciously. Professional land speculators differ from other land owners in the periphery primarily in that they are motivated more exclusively by this consideration. Hence they are more likely to leave land untended and uncultivated while they are waiting for a rise in price. Or, if they cultivate it, they are more likely to favor those forms of agriculture that require the least investment in labor, buildings, or machinery. Examples include grain farming and grazing. The existence of such professional speculation is one of the main reasons that idle land or extensively cultivated grain fields can be found adjacent to land used intensively to raise crops or animals. Of course, the role of land speculation could be reduced by appropriate changes in tax policies, but there does not seem much interest in this around most metropolitan areas.

The repelling forces I have been describing are more evident around American metropolitan areas than in other developed economies, partly because of our greater affluence and partly because of less rigid regulation of land use. In America, on the metropolitan frontier, land is considered limitless, just as it was considered limitless during the westward movement. In countries such as England, with less land and less of the pioneering tradition, land is more often considered finite, and hence its use is more heavily regulated. However, despite these differences, the same repelling effects can be noted in nearly all developed economies.

The Resolution of Attracting and Repelling Forces

In a hypothetical situation, the opposing forces of attraction and repulsion might reach some sort of equilibrium pattern in which there would be definite zones of different land uses. That is, an equilibrium pattern would be possible if the strengths of the opposing forces remained stable and essentially the same for long periods. But in the real world, the metropolis and the metropolitan economy are highly dynamic, and hence the opposing locational forces are too subject to change, or waxing and waning in strength, to permit more than the most tentative of fixed locational patterns to emerge.

Further, equilibrium in this locational system is retarded by inertia. Inertia often tends to keep a given property in a previous land use long after the strength of the earlier locational forces has markedly changed. Partly, this is a matter of the economic costs of conversion. For example, farmland that has reverted to brush may be too expensive to clear again for farming. Or, land once laid out in residential lots may be too expensive to recombine into the larger parcels needed for farms, manufacturing sites, or suburban shopping sites. Sometimes overcoming the legal red tape in assembling properties is a greater economic obstacle than a hill might be.

But often the inertia is cultural or social in origin. For example, there is an area within the political borders of Cincinnati known as Dutch Hollow. It is an area of open land and greenhouses operated by a closely knit community of German-American farmers surrounded by the general urban development of Cincinnati. It is a locational survival from the time when the area was on the periphery of developing Cincinnati. In the usual situation, the repelling forces would have long since pushed such production farther out into the present-day metropolitan periphery. Though many factors appear to be involved in this special case, it seems clear that the cultural cohesion of the community was an important factor in its survival.

Other examples could be cited for other metropolitan areas. On the national scene, perhaps the best single example of such sociocultural resistance to the repelling force of the metropolis is the Pennsylvania Dutch area of Pennsylvania. There, flourishing farms are found much closer to the metropolitan areas than is generally the case. Little farmland has been allowed to revert to wasteland. Factories are common in the zone, but they are well hidden, blended into the supposedly rural landscape.

In short, the locational pattern in the metropolitan periphery today is unstable, somewhat unpredictable, irregular, and spotty. The locational resolution of the opposing forces of attraction and repulsion varies from time to time and from metropolis to metropolis. Around specific metropolitan areas it is possible to observe some tendencies toward circular zonations reflecting the strengths of the opposing forces at a point in time. There is no geographic riddle more fascinating than the attempt to discern such zonations for a particular metropolis, to reconstruct past zonations from old maps and photographs, or to guess what the resolution of the opposing forces will produce in geographic patterns in the next year or the next decade.

CHAPTER 6

The Metropolis as a Spatial Production System

Preceding chapters have described contemporary locational patterns for the metropolis in terms of specific forms of production: services (Chapter 3), manufacturing (Chapter 4), and primary production (Chapter 5). Each has been described separately in order to simplify the discussion. Obviously, that is not enough. It is only a beginning. For the most significant aspect of the metropolis is that it is a vast, intricate system of interacting forms of production, housing, and people. Every production site is linked with thousands of other production sites in a vast locational web. In addition to the linkages existing at any one moment in time, every production site is *potentially* linkable with every other production site in the metropolis or its periphery; an almost infinite number of spatial arrangements is conceivable. Some of these potential linkages will be realized as the metropolis grows and changes over time, discarding old spatial arrangements and accepting new ones. Others will remain forever as potentials only, because the technology needed to make them practical does not emerge, or because individual metropolitans are not adventurous enough to dream of the almost infinite possibilities open to them in a dynamic, creative economy, or because there is too much cultural resistance to spatial change.

This vast spatial web of the production system of the metropolis and its periphery is self-adjusting and self-regulating, within limits. That is to say, changes in one part of this spatial complex tend to create pressures for change in other parts of the system. For example, as people begin to disperse into the metropolitan periphery, services begin to follow them, and manufacturing, too. Or does manufacturing lead and the others follow? Or are all of these movements so closely related as to be almost simultaneous, mutually supporting, locational decisions, a general response to declining accessibility within the metropolis (increasing congestion) and increasing accessibility on its borders?

But this metropolitan dispersal produces social pressures from the poor packed in the inner portions of the metropolis; *their* accessibility to potential jobs has been reduced by automation and the shift of some jobs to the metropolitan periphery. So there are attempts to upgrade education for the poor and attempts to move some jobs back to the ghettos or to provide better transportation between ghettos and peripheral jobs. And so it goes. Yes, this spatial system is partially self-adjusting and self-regulating. But the possibility of its being self-regulating is closely related to the adequacy of the spatial information generally available, to the information the system itself collects about the continuing changes going on in this vast, intricate, spatial web.

The spatial changes going on daily or yearly in the metropolis, not considering the spatial changes that may occur in a decade, are almost more than a single mind can grasp. But a computer, if programmed with sufficient sophistication, can reduce the multitudinous changes to general trends and tendencies that are more easily dealt with. Spatial changes have meaning particularly in relation to shifts away from previous patterns and shifts toward patterns we do not yet know; the memory banks of computers can store *accurate* information about past spatial patterns, unclouded by human tendencies toward nostalgia. But a computer can be no more useful than the programs written for it and no more useful than the information fed into it.

Obviously, the time span between the federal censuses is too great to catch many of the spatial changes in the metropolis in time to do anything about them. It is a bit like deciding whether or not to go swimming in Lake Michigan on the basis of temperature readings taken every five or ten years. Therefore, many metropolitan areas in the United States are now developing so-called Urban Data Banks. These involve the frequent reporting, collating, and storing of locationally coded information from all those groups or individuals who wish to share in the common pool of information. For example, such a group might include manufacturers, retail chains, utilities companies, real estate groups, transportation firms or agencies, welfare agencies, educational groups, those planning medical facilities, and so on. Meanwhile, urban planners and others with a special interest in the spatial patterns of the metropolis, such as geographers, are trying to develop computer programs with sufficient sophistication to be useful.

Though such computer programs are useful to specialists now, and will no doubt be even more useful in the future, they are not very helpful to those with a more general interest in the metropolis and overall locational trends in the economy, such as the readers of this book. For such purposes, one needs a very simplified schematic diagram, a diagram of the metropolis that can be readily grasped and that can be of some help in interpreting the metropolis as one sees it with one's own eyes. The average educated citizen of the metropolis needs a simplified diagram of the metropolis, which he can carry in his head, and against which he can plot changes occurring or changes urged by those with metropolitan planning as their full-time responsibility. The purpose of this chapter is to provide such a simplified, schematic view of the metropolis and its periphery. Such a view has its uses in interpreting the metropolis itself; it is also useful in interpreting the geography of the whole economy insofar as the metropolis is in fact a mirror of the economy (see subsequent chapters).

Before getting into a discussion of schematic diagrams of the metropolis that do exist, I need to discuss briefly an aspect of the geography of the metropolis that has received very little attention so far in this book. It has received very little attention here only because geographers have just recently begun to make really sophisticated analyses of it, not because it is unimportant to an interpretation of the metropolis. Indeed, it is probably the most important single clue to understanding the spatial web of the metropolis: a geographic or spatial interpretation of the transportation and communications network. A great deal is known about such networks and how they relate to spatial decision-making. But most of this information is diffuse and poorly organized. It is only recently that geographers have begun to develop models of such networks which sort the divergent tendencies out so that they can be clearly recognized.

At some future time, when metropolitan transportation networks are better understood, most of the locational models presented in previous chapters will need to be thoroughly overhauled and modified. For, quite obviously, locational decision-making in the metropolis involves not only specific sites for production (the main emphasis in preceding chapters), but also the nature of the geometry of linkages among sites and potential sites. But, in the meantime, let us consider some existing schematic diagrams of the metropolis: the concentric ring model, the sector model, and the multiple nuclei model.

The Concentric Ring Model

The concentric ring model was one of the earliest attempts to develop a simple, schematic diagram of the metropolitan areas, which were becoming a more and more common phenomenon in the late nineteenth and early twentieth centuries. The many schematic diagrams of real or utopian cities of earlier times quite obviously were drawn with something much smaller, less dynamic, and less complex than the modern metropolis in mind. This model (Figure 1A) was initially developed in Chicago, with Chicago as the prototype, about half a century ago. Since then it has been much interpreted, reinterpreted, and modified in various ways. Drawn before metropolitan dispersal was a major phenomenon, it includes only the metropolis proper and does not include the area beyond, discussed in Chapter 5. The general thesis of the model is very similar to the von Thunen model for agricultural production (see Chapters 5 and 9). That is, like the von Thunen model, it

FIGURE 1: *Models of Metropolitan Form*

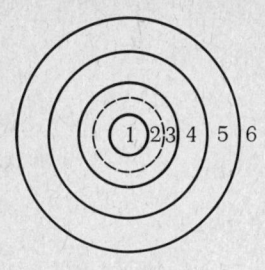

A. Concentric Rings

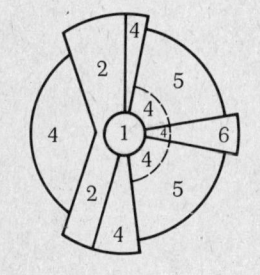

B. Sectors or Wedges

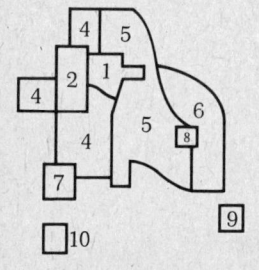

C. Multiple Nuclei

1. Central Business District
2. Wholesaling and Light Manufacturing
3. Transitional Zone
4. Residential Zone, Low Income
5. Residential Zone, Middle Income
6. Residential Zone, High Income
7. Heavy Manufacturing
8. Satellite Business District
9. Suburb, Residential
10. Suburb, Industrial

The diagrams are modified versions of those initially appearing in Park, Burgess, and McKenzie, eds., *The City*, 1925, pp. 51–53, and in Harris and Ullman, *Annals of the American Academy of Political and Social Science*, Vol. 242 (1945), p. 13.

is a land-use or land-rent model, which assumes that the location of production is primarily a function of land costs. And, like it, it assumes that land costs are primarily determined by accessibility to a single, central point. In the von Thunen model, the central point is the city, which is the market for the farm production. In the model by Burgess (the concentric ring model), the central point is the CBD.

It is easy to criticize the model as being oversimplified and no doubt it is. But it is quite correct in stressing the importance of accessibility in the metropolitan system, even though this accessibility is shown only as accessibility to the central point rather than as a more complex matter of accessibility to a transportation network. Likewise, it is quite correct in stressing the dynamism of a metropolitan system, even though this dynamism is indicated only in terms of the effect of expanding functions in the inner rings on the displacement of functions into outer rings. Clearly, this expansion-displacement effect occurs in other ways and in other places, too. The frequent criticism that the model does not include the effect of topographic differences on the system is not valid. To include all of the topographic variety found in every metropolis would be too confusing. Instead, specific topographic differences in a specific metropolis should be taken into account when trying to apply the model to that particular area. Similarly, the specific histories of every metropolis, including the location of the nuclei for ghetto formation, are too diverse to be included. In attempting to fit the model to a specific metropolis, such local variations must be taken into account.

Basically, the model assumes that the location of production is a function of land costs, which, in turn, are a function of distance from a central point, the CBD. That is, the model assumes a cone of land costs such as that described in Chapter 4—highest at the center and gradually diminishing in all directions. Land costs are assumed to be highest in the CBD because that is the most accessible point and therefore there is the greatest competition for space there. Just as in the von Thunen model, it assumes that different kinds of producers have different needs for accessibility. Hence, they will tend to sort themselves out into productive rings around the central point according to these accessibility needs.

Those functions that have the greatest need for accessibility (for example, retailing) will bid up the price of the land until they can obtain the most central sites; others who need accessibility almost as badly (manufacturers such as publishers and brewers) will accept slightly lower-priced sites in a ring just outside the CBD. The lower-paid workers (such as factory workers and some employees of retailers), who need to be close to their work to reduce commuting costs, will locate in a ring just beyond the factory ring, even though land is expensive there, too. But the high price of the land is offset in part by crowding in housing, trading limited living space for nearness to employment and services. The high price of the land is also offset in part by the age and obsolescence of the housing in this zone. The workers who live in the outer rings have the least expensive land; they are able to pay the higher commuting costs and in exchange get more living space.

But the model does not assume a static cone of land costs. It assumes, instead, that the metropolis is growing in population and production. Therefore, as the CBD expands, it displaces part of the manufacturing ring into the worker ring, part of the worker ring into the commuter ring, and part of the commuter ring into the countryside. It should be noted that this involves the assumption that all expansion is *horizontal*. In actual fact, in the last century, much of the service expansion of the CBD has been *vertical* rather than horizontal; it has been upward into higher and higher skyscrapers more than it has been outward into surrounding rings. Meanwhile, the multistory vertical factory layout so characteristic of metropolitan manufacturing in the past has frequently changed to a horizontal, one-story layout, which might be uneconomic in the inner ring shown in the model, but which is quite economic on the outer edges of the metropolitan system.

Obviously, the model is oversimplified, but it clarifies by its very simplicity. Land prices *are* highest in the CBD, they do tend to decrease away from it (though not nearly so regularly as indicated in the model), they do tend to sort out different forms of production into bands or zones, and they do tend to change over time, modifying the whole system. Of course, other factors affect the system, too, so it is not quite that simple.

The Sector Model

The sector or wedge model of Homer Hoyt (Figure 1B) was first elaborated in 1939. It retains the basic land rent assumptions of the concentric ring model, but adds two special factors: (1) the effect of *linear accessibility*, or radial transport routes, and (2) the effects of *directional inertia*, or the tendency for early developments on the periphery of the CBD to be retained and extended outward as the system expands over time. As in the concentric ring model, it seems that the metropolis is growing primarily horizontally rather than vertically. Like that model, the sector model stresses the role of accessibility. But this stress includes not only the general accessibility relating to one point (the CBD), but also, somewhat more realistically, ridges of moderate accessibility extending along the radial transport routes. The accessibility cone, as conceived in this model, is no longer a smooth cone; now, it is a cone with ridges of added accessibility extending down the cone.

It should be noted that the manufacturing wedge, as well as other wedges, is oriented to such an accessibility ridge rather than being ringed around the CBD, as in the concentric ring model. However, as discussed in Chapter 4, two different kinds of manufacturing may be involved. There is one type of manufacturing that favors a location peripheral to the CBD and a somewhat different type that favors location along major transport routes. Clearly, an adequate schematic diagram for the metropolis must take *all* major types into account. However, the limitations of the model should not be overstressed. The leap from thinking of accessibility only in terms of a point, to thinking of accessibility also in terms of a line is an important leap. It is a leap in the direction of a diagram of the metropolis that includes whole transport networks, as discussed previously in this chapter.

Homer Hoyt was particularly interested in the location of housing. Perhaps that is what led him to include the concept of *directional inertia*. The effects of this can be noted in many aspects of the metropolis, but they seem particularly evident in housing. The basic idea is that custom and social snobbery tend to perpetuate initial housing patterns. If a particular side of town (side of the CBD) becomes associated in the public mind with the wealthy, this influences subsequent housing choices. The wealthy (and the not-so-wealthy social climbers) may tend to congregate in that area; as the metropolis grows, the area extends outward and becomes one of the wedges making up the metropolis. Similarly, areas of low-income housing may be extended outward as wedges. There seems to be considerable truth in this. However, it must also be remembered that the aging and obsolescence of housing also influences housing choice and this tends to support ringlike patterns rather than wedge patterns. No doubt both tendencies are real.

The stress laid by Homer Hoyt on social imagery is appropriate, quite apart from its specific connection with the idea of directional inertia. That locational decisions are made in terms of simplified images people carry in their heads is quite true. And, that these images are often important in shaping the metropolis is also true. For a contemporary example, note the support of urban renewal efforts for a particular service geography (see Chapter 3). In short, diverse locational choices in the metropolis are being made not only *simultaneously* (choices about services, manufacturing, primary production, and housing being made together rather than separately, as has been stressed repeatedly in this chapter), but also *sequentially* (choices being influenced by individual and social attitudes about the locational choices that have been previously made).

The Multiple Nuclei Model

The excessive simplicities of these models have encouraged others to develop more elaborate models. Perhaps the best known of these is the multiple nuclei model of Harris and Ullman (1945). Their diagram (Figure 1C) is only suggestive of actual locations in any specific metropolis; the overall matrix is what is important rather than the specific places assigned to particular functions. The model assumes that functional areas or "economic cells" would emerge in any metropolis, but the relative size of each such area and the particular geometric relationship among the areas would be unpredictable except in terms of the specific topography and economic history of the particular metropolis. Others, in turn, have sought to modify and elaborate the original Harris and Ullman diagram. The following discussion is in general harmony with the ideas of Harris and Ullman, but does involve some modifications.

The key idea is that the metropolis is thought of as being multicellular rather than only unicellular. Both the Burgess model and the Hoyt model are unicellular; that is, one point (the CBD) is assumed to control the whole system. But in the Harris and Ullman diagram it is assumed that in addition to the major economic cell (the system as a whole focusing on the CBD), there are also lesser economic cells scattered through the system. Why and how do these lesser cells form? They form around growth points or "nuclei" within the general urbanizing zone. Often these growth points or nuclei are the historical residue of pre-metropolitan patterns. For example, what becomes the CBD of the metropolis may begin simply as the chief city of a rural zone in which a central place pattern (towns, villages, and hamlets) has developed in the manner described in Chapters 3 and 7. These settlements, or some of them, may become growth points in the emerging metropolitan system. But other growth points may also emerge, perhaps linked to the emerging metropolitan transport network, or to the locational pattern emerging for manufacturing (see Chapter 4), or to the diverse service patterns discussed in Chapter 3. Still other economic cells in the system are not so much growth points as they are filler in the pattern; they fill in the spaces not preempted by the functions more associated with growth points. For example, the cheaper housing developments may be of this filler type.

Accessibility is involved in the development of growth points, whether one thinks of a single growth point (the CBD) or many growth points of varying potency. In this, all three models agree. But the concentric ring model and the sector model consider only *positive accessibility*, the desirability of access. The Harris and Ullman model includes also *negative accessibility*, the deliberate choosing of a site that is not readily accessible to some other metropolitan function. For example, expensive housing is often located as far away as possible from unattractive forms of manufacturing; cheaper housing or other metropolitan functions may be located in between and provide a buffer of sorts. In short, sometimes differing functions *repel* each other as well as attracting each other.

According to this model, the accessibility cone of the other two models is seen as a series of cones resting on the sides of a major cone or as a mountainous area with a single central peak dominating the others. The location of the lesser cones is seen as partially a function of the transport network (as with the sectors of the Hoyt model), but also as a function of the area's history and the potency of the locational mix at each of these growth points. The system is assumed to be dynamic, as in the other models, but in a more complex way. It is assumed that low-cost housing tends to occupy the low-rent spaces between the cones, or growth points. However, these spaces may also be occupied by the more economically marginal forms of services or manufacturing. By economically marginal, I mean those that would disappear if forced to use more expensive sites in the growth points. Firms with such narrow profit margins would include both old firms struggling to survive and new, beginning firms with limited capital.

Of course, the spaces occupied by such cheap housing or economically marginal firms may be former growth points left behind in the shifting accessibility pattern of the metropolis. In many ways, such zones in the metropolis (slums, blighted areas, and so on) are analogous to the much larger depressed areas (such as Appalachia) that can be observed in the national economy. Like them, they are "in" the economy in a physical sense, but not fully "of" the economy in a functional sense. The degree to which such an analogy is actually valid will be discussed in Chapter 10.

Beyond These Models

It is easy to criticize all three diagrams as being excessively simplistic. Any diagram that includes every significant factor affecting the locational pattern of the metropolis is likely to become so complicated and cluttered that it is of little value to anyone except its author. But *he* may learn a lot attempting to draw it. Accordingly, the reader is invited to draw his own diagram. Should the reader be unable to contain his pride in his handiwork, he should send me a copy. If it expresses precisely the right balance between oversimplification and excessive complexity, I promise to use it in my next book!

The aspects of the metropolitan pattern highlighted in the three models are no doubt true, as far as they go; so no doubt they should be included in the improved diagram. But if the reader feels as I do that they do not go far enough, then some means should be found to add other locational aspects of the metropolis diagrammatically. These might well include more attention to transport networks, a greater variety of service patterns (arterial developments, ribbon developments, and specialized functional zones as well as central place patterns), a greater variety of manufacturing patterns (concentrations on highway radials and suburban clusters as well as the CBD fringe and railroad-waterfront concentrations), general tendencies toward the flattening of the Central Place System and toward metropolitan dispersal, some aspects of the land-use confusion resulting from attraction-repulsion in the fifty-mile peripheral zone, the possibilities of a vertical expression of growth as well as a horizontal expression of that growth, and the significance of industrial slums and commercial slums as well as housing slums.

Of course, no diagram can show many of the most crucial aspects of the geography of the metropolis. For example, the role of perception. There is always a discrepancy between the reality of the spatial pattern of the metropolis and the image of the metropolis people carry in their heads. Yet it is on the basis of such images that spatial decisions are made, either by individuals or planning groups. Changes in such images require feedback, new impressions of the reality of the metropolis derived from ordinary daily experience, from the newspapers and other media reporting on the metropolis, and from more sophisticated sources such as Urban Data Banks. Yet such informational feedback is always imperfect, and, in any case, we like to cling to established imagery. So our images of the metropolis always involve certain archaic elements, certain aspects of a rear-view-mirror vision of our metropolitan world. Hopefully, the image of the metropolis presented in these chapters is less archaic than most and therefore provides a valid basis not only for interpreting the present-day metropolis, but also the geography of larger areas discussed in following chapters.

PART III

The Metropolis Writ Large: The Economic Geography of Developed Countries

CHAPTER 7

Service Geography Beyond the Metropolis

So far, I have stressed production *within* the metropolis itself. This is important to do because such a large proportion of all economic production now occurs in metropolitan areas. However, the individual metropolis does not stand alone. A modern, metropolitan economy consists of more than a few metropolitan areas scattered indiscriminately, unrelated to each other in space. The individual metropolis is simply a node in the overall locational network, the overall production complex. On the one hand, the individual metropolis is the principal node in a spatial system of production that includes all of the cities, towns, villages, and hamlets within the trading area or hinterland of the metropolis. The farming, forestry, mining, recreation, manufacturing, and services produced in that hinterland are linked spatially with each other through the transportation network and the system of central places. Generally, this spatial system focuses on the principal node in that system of central places, the metropolis. In short, a metropolitan economy involves more than just the metropolis itself; it also includes the hinterland of that metropolis.

On the other hand, one should not think of each metropolis and its hinterland as a separate and discrete economic cell, unrelated to other metropolitan areas and their hinterlands. Instead, the various metropolitan areas, with their hinterlands, are themselves linked together in still larger spatial systems of production involving whole nations, groups of nations, and in some cases global networks of production.

The purpose of this chapter, and following chapters, is to examine the location of production in this wider framework, this different scale of areas many times larger than individual metropolitan areas. This book is organized around the idea that in many ways the metropolis is a mirror of the locational patterns of the whole economy. Therefore, analogies with the metropolitan area will be used wherever appropriate to make the locational pattern of production understandable. However, the best of mirrors usually involves some distortion. Therefore, wherever there seem to be significant deviations away from patterns found within the metropolis itself, these will be pointed out.

This specific chapter considers only one aspect of that wider pattern of production, the location of services. Subsequent chapters deal with other aspects of such production patterns: manufacturing, mining, agriculture, and the linkages among all forms of production. The geography of services alone is a highly complex matter. Consider first the relatively simple patterns at one end of this chain of increasing complexity, those involved in the relation of the handful of stores and other institutions (such as churches and schools) in a hamlet or crossroads to their immediate service area or hinterland. It is not only that the area served is small, only a few square miles. It is also that the number of linkages from the homes in the area to the hamlet are rather modest; just a few services are provided. And it is also that these linkages are relatively obvious and easily comprehensible to all concerned. Villages provide more services than hamlets, and their hinterlands are larger, more complex, and less comprehensible. However, their patterns are still simple enough so that there is no great mystery about them, except, perhaps, in detail.

But when one moves upward to a much larger network, such as the network of hamlets, villages, towns, small cities, and cities in the hinterland of a metropolis, one is dealing with a highly complex pattern that is not necessarily obvious or readily comprehensible to the inhabitants. Such networks rival in complexity the service geography of the metropolis itself. If one moves, then, into still larger and more complex service systems such as those of whole nations, the problem of understanding becomes more difficult still. The service hinterland of New York City is perhaps the most complex in the world. It is nearly global in extent, involves a great many services that are of such a sophisticated nature (such as international finance or investment banking) that they are difficult to measure and record, and includes a great number of individual metropolitan areas and their hinterlands with all of *their* complexities.

Great centers such as New York tend to attract the top talent of the time, people with great natural abilities, good educations, highly developed expertise, and wide-ranging minds. Yet I can say with no fear of contradiction that there is no single living person who truly understands the service geography focusing on New York in all its complexities and ambiguities. And if the forces unleashed by the Second Agglomerative Revolution continue in vigor, this will be more and more true in the future, unless some kind of super-super-intellect emerges. The hypothetical metropolis discussed in preceding chapters is more or less midway on this chain of increasing complexity in service geography from a hamlet to New York. This is one of the reasons the metropolis was discussed first, before the more complex patterns considered in this chapter. In this chapter, the simpler patterns, those in the hinterland of the metropolis, are discussed first. Then, the question of linkages among metropolitan areas themselves is considered.

The Service Hinterland of the Metropolis

How can one come to understand the essential geographic pattern in the network of services focusing on the metropolis? Obviously, there is nothing quite as useful as actual observation. Armchair theorizing is certainly useful, but actual observation is essential to check on the theorizing and to keep it from becoming an end in itself. But *which* metropolitan hinterland should we observe? Clearly, for a general understanding of such patterns one must seek out a hinterland with as few distortions away from the general case as possible. For example, the hinterland of Los Angeles has many special geographic characteristics related to the predominance of desert and mountain land in that hinterland. Montreal is a special case, too, since so much of its hinterland is forested, non-agricultural, and thinly populated. Then, what of Pittsburgh? Pittsburgh's hinterland is certainly not typical because the population is so heavily industrial and because it is distributed in rather special ways due to the hilliness of the land, the pattern of coal seams, and so on. The hinterlands of very few metropolitan areas are without significant special geographic aspects; one could not hope to develop a general understanding of service geography from studying one such metropolitan area alone. One answer to this problem is to study them all, and from that to derive the general case. But time and space do not permit that here.

Yes, the real world *is* complicated. However, within the Middle West, particularly in the Corn Belt and the eastern parts of the Wheat Belt, the general geography is relatively uncomplicated. Furthermore, the general nature of the Middle West is likely to be known to most of the readers of this book, so that the reader himself can provide some of the complicating details not included here. Broadly speaking, there are few natural barriers to transportation or communication in the Middle West. There is a general uniformity in the quality of the land. Though average temperatures decrease from south to north and average rainfall decreases from east to west, there are few abrupt climatic changes. Though soils do vary in fertility, there is a general tendency toward great similarity for broad areas. A high proportion of the land is cultivated; though forested patches exist, they generally do not distort the service patterns a great deal.

The general uniformity over broad areas extends to the culture of the people as well. Most of the Middle West was settled by much the same kind of people over a relatively short historical period under basically similar legal, political, and economic conditions. Generally, the farmers settled on the land on holdings of similar size, rather than concentrating in residential villages as was common during the First Agglomerative Revolution. Throughout the area, the farmers today tend to have comparable educations, knowledge of farming techniques, and income expectations. This general uniformity of a Middle West hinterland is disrupted here and there by mining and manufacturing. The distribution of these activities is much more irregular than the distribution of agriculture. Still, much of the manufacturing outside metropolitan areas is linked to the local environment, that is, linked to the processing of farm products or to the manufacturing of products for the local population. So the distribution of manufacturing is not as disruptive of the general pattern of uniformity as it might be. In any case, there is no better place in which to avoid excessive geographic complexities, and yet to examine a real situation.

So let us assume that our hypothetical metropolis is located in the Corn Belt. The service patterns in the hinterlands of the metropolitan areas of the Corn Belt have been studied exhaustively, not only in terms of actual observation, but also in terms of detailed analyses of collected data. These studies show that the general pattern is broadly similar to the Central Place System described for the hypothetical metropolis. The lowest-order Central Places are the hamlets or crossroads centers selling such items as gasoline, cigarettes, bread, milk, and routine groceries. Currently, the hamlets are tending to die out, just as the lower levels of the Central Place System of the metropolis have declined somewhat in favor of larger service clusters. The hamlets that show the greatest tendency toward survival seem to be those located on major highways. It is apparent that their survival is linked to an increasing dependency on transit trade which offsets the decline in local trade. Thus, their essential nature, though not necessarily their appearance, comes more and more to resemble the ribbon developments of the metropolis.

The next higher order Central Place, the village, shows some of the same tendencies toward ribboning and the transit function, but it remains rather more viable in the Central Place sense. As studied specifically by Brian Berry in southwestern Iowa (a portion of the hinterland of Omaha-Council Bluffs), the typical village has services such as those provided by groceries, bars, gas stations, restaurants, post offices, farm elevators, and churches. Usually, there are between 30 and 40 such separate establishments. The village serves between 1,000 and 1,200 people, of whom about 500 live in the village proper and between 500 and 700 live in the surrounding farming zone. The apparent maximum range for a village is about 5 miles; hence, the total area served is about 70 square miles.

There are not as many towns as there are villages and they are spaced farther apart. A town provides all of the services found in a hamlet or village, but also some not found in those places. In southwestern Iowa, added types of services typically include a hardware store, furniture and appliance store, drugstore, dry cleaner, bank, funeral parlor, and such specialists as doctor, dentist, and insurance agent. As many as 50 different *kinds* of businesses may exist in as many as 90 or 100 separate establishments. The population actually residing in the town may vary from about 1,200 upward to around 1,700. The maximum range of the town exceeds that of the village. It is about 8 miles, so that a market area of about 200 square miles is tapped, rather than only about 70 square miles. This means more customers. So perhaps about 4,000 people may be served from the town, including 1,200 to 1,700 in the town proper and the rest on farms or in the hamlets or villages within that 200 square miles.

But a population of 4,000 people is still not large enough to reach the thresholds of some other kinds of service establishments not found in the town. For example, shoe stores, jewelry stores, clothing stores, auto sales, movie theaters, and the like. So for such specialization, the inhabitants of the villages and towns and their surrounding farming population must travel farther away to a small city. The small cities of southwestern Iowa, as defined by Brian Berry, have resident populations of 6,400 to 6,900. Their ranges extend for almost 20 miles so that each taps a trading area of as much as 1,000 square miles and perhaps 20,000 people (farmers and the inhabitants of hamlets, villages, and towns). The resident population plus this surrounding population gives a gross population to be served of 25,000 to 30,000 people. With this economic base, a small city provides all of the goods and services provided in the smaller centers (hamlets, villages, and towns) and more. As many as 100 *kinds* of businesses may be found in the small city, distributed in as many as 300 to 400 separate establishments.

But if the inhabitants of such an area seek a still higher level of services or a greater variety of services, they must travel farther, to a regional city such as Council Bluffs, or to a metropolis such as Omaha (actually, Council Bluffs and Omaha are almost merged, forming one great metropolis). For example, the inhabitants of the area may wish to patronize a department store. The range of Omaha-Council Bluffs extends for at least 40 miles into Iowa and presumably similar distances into Nebraska in the other direction. The resulting size of the population served, both within Omaha-Council Bluffs and within this large trade area, greatly exceeds that of the small city. The total population served is great enough to meet more thresholds and hence to allow a greater variety of services and more specialized or higher-level ones.

Such a geographic distribution of services seems to be close to the general case for the hinterlands of metropolitan areas in the developed world. Variations away from such a pattern are often found, of course, based on peculiar local circumstances in the distribution of the population, income, or cultural characteristics. To what extent is such a pattern like or different from the service pattern discussed in Chapter 3 *within* the metropolis? A principal difference is the rather obvious one that because the population is less dense, the distances between any two Central Places at the same rank in the hierarchy are much greater in the rural area than in the metropolis. Another notable difference is that there seems to be somewhat more regularity in the pattern in rural Iowa, with its relatively evenly spaced consuming population, than in the metropolis with its wide variations in population density and income levels. Still another apparent difference is that the differences among the levels of the hierarchy (hamlets, villages, towns, small cities, and so on) seem sharper and easier to discern than the comparable hierarchical levels in the metropolis (corner store, neighborhood shopping area, regional shopping area, and CBD), where they tend at least visually to merge together more.

But though there are quite definitely differences in the two patterns, there are also significant similarities. In the Central Place patterns of both areas there are (1) a successive parceling of the whole area into a hierarchy of Central Places, (2) a distinction in levels in the hierarchies (the hamlet-village-town-small city sequence paralleling the neighborhood regional center-CBD sequence), (3) a very close relationship between the range or trade area of the Central Place and the variety and level of goods and services provided at that place, and (4) a close relationship between the location of the lower-order centers and those above them in the hierarchy.

The discovery that such regularities in service geography do exist and that they can be analyzed despite the inevitable variations produced by differences in the general geography of an area has led to attempts to measure these regularities mathematically and geometrically. Such precision is highly useful in some contexts, but goes beyond the modest aims of this book. Readers interested in such detailed mathematical and geometric treatment should consult a recent book by Brian Berry, *Geography of Market Centers and Retail Distributions*, which provided the raw material for much of the discussion here about southwestern Iowa.

But what of change in the service geography of metropolitan hinterlands? In Chapter 3, I stressed the fact that change was a basic aspect of the metropolis. Is that not also true of the hinterlands? Indeed it is. In both the metropolis and its hinterland, there is evidence of a "selective thinning" of the Central Place System, particularly at the lower levels of the hierarchy. Nearly everywhere in the hinterland the higher-order centers seem to be growing at the expense of the lower centers as accessibility increases, that is, as transportation improves. In such selective thinning, it appears that the regional shopping centers located on the fringes of the metropolis are the most general winners. That is, they seem to be growing both at the expense of their chief metropolitan rival (the CBD) *and* at the expense of some of the centers in the hinterland. However, this is a relatively recent development, and has not been analyzed in sufficient detail for us to be certain of its significance.

Beyond changes in the Central Place System itself, both the metropolis and its hinterland show the emergence of ribbon developments, though in the metropolis this usually means the addition of new service establishments whereas in the hinterland it often means simply the continuation of hamlets and villages along highways that otherwise might be selectively thinned out. However, two other recent variations on the Central Place System of the metropolis, nodal arterial developments and specialized functional zones, have not generally emerged in the metropolitan hinterland. Perhaps they will, but it seems doubtful because a large population is needed to support such specialized types of service patterns.

Service Networks Among Metropolitan Areas

It is quite evident that there are differing degrees of specialization among metropolitan areas and that there is some degree of geographic ordering or patterning of the service linkages among metropolitan areas. For example, although Cincinnati is the chief service center in its region or hinterland, it is clear that it is dependent to some degree on more specialized service centers such as New York. Presumably, the service geography of large areas, involving many metropolitan areas, is basically similar to the service geography of the metropolis or its hinterland, just more complicated. Presumably, the basic concepts of range, threshold, and hierarchy are universally applicable in service geography.

However, service relationships among metropolitan areas have not been studied with the same thoroughness that they have been studied for smaller areas such as metropolitan hinterlands. In part, this is because service geography is much more complicated at this higher level. In addition, the higher one proceeds in the service hierarchy, the fewer the number of cases on which to build generalizations and the greater the chances of error. In a country as large as the

United States, there are thousands of villages about which to generalize. But there is only one New York, one metropolitan area that is preeminent over all other metropolitan areas. So it is hard to tell how much the service patterns of New York are due to unique historical and geographic circumstances and how much they are simply the product of the overall size and vitality of the economic areas served by New York. In short, the specific comments here about the service linkages among metropolitan areas are offered with a little less certainty and a little more hesitation than those offered earlier in the book. But, by now, the reader should welcome a little humility on the part of the author!

Though there seem to be hierarchical steps among the levels of services offered by the various metropolitan areas, these steps are not as clear as those for smaller centers. However, the pattern is probably something like that shown in Table 1. New York clearly belongs in first rank. It is the pre-

TABLE 1: A HYPOTHETICAL SERVICE HIERARCHY

A. Metropolitan Central Places

1. Supranational Centers
   EXAMPLE: *New York*
2. National Service Centers and Major Sub-national Centers
   EXAMPLES: *Milan, Chicago*
3. Sub-national Service Centers
   EXAMPLES: *Cleveland, St. Louis, Atlanta*
4. Lesser Sub-national Service Centers
   EXAMPLES: *Pittsburgh, Cincinnati, Seattle*
5. Regional Centers and all lesser Metropolitan Areas
   EXAMPLES: *Dayton, Ohio; Lexington, Kentucky*

B. Nonmetropolitan Central Places

6. *Small City*
7. *Town*
8. *Village*
9. *Hamlet or Crossroads*

eminent service center for the United States even though it has a strong competitor in Washington, D.C., for one class of services, governmental services. For example, New York is the center of the Federal Reserve Banking System, which "manages" the whole economy under rules laid down by Congress by controlling money and credit flows.

The majority of the really large corporations of the United States have their headquarters in New York. Large corporations are closely regulated by the government and they perform many quasi-governmental functions such as tax collection (withholding taxes). In addition, New York is the largest single insurance center and has the greatest variety of insurance services. It is the principal center for the spread of ideas and the molding of public opinion (news, information, publishing, public relations, advertising, and so on). Many of the larger metropolitan areas of the United States have stock exchanges, but the stock exchanges of New York are overwhelmingly larger in volume and variety than any others in the United States. Historically, the concentration of stock exchanges there was linked with banking, insurance, and corporate headquarters functions, but today the linkage with New York as an idea center and news center may be more significant, for the buying and selling of stock today is closely linked to mass psychology.

Even if New York had no international role, it would be a truly impressive service center because the United States accounts for a significant proportion of all world production, including services. But, in addition, New York has a major supranational role. It provides banking services and insurance services for a large part of the Noncommunist World, particularly for the Western Hemisphere. The headquarters of many major international corporations in New York provide economic planning and management advice for subsidiaries in nearly all parts of the so-called Free World. In the developed countries this often involves particularly manufacturing and retailing, as in Western Europe. In the less developed parts of the world this more often involves mining and transportation development. In recent decades, New York's role as a supranational service center has been expanding more rapidly than its role as a national service center.

The general tendency for the higher-level services to become more and more concentrated in fewer and fewer centers, such as New York, is probably just another example of the trend toward the selective thinning of service centers with improvements in transportation and communication. The inhabitants of other service centers threatened by this trend can be expected to fight back with any means at their disposal, just as the merchants of a village may appeal to local loyalties and the like in order to try to protect themselves from the increasing competition of the merchants in the town. But, within nations, the merchants may lack political means to gain their ends. In the case of supranational service centers, international politics plays a significant role. The fulminations of the Soviet bloc against Wall Street can be understood in this light, though of course the international services of New York are by no means all concentrated in Wall Street. Similarly, de Gaulle's concern over the success of American corporate management in Europe was, in many respects, a resistance to the rise of New York as the preeminent supranational service center.

New York has a number of competitors as a supranational service center. Certainly, London and Moscow are competitors. London not only dominates the service geography of Great Britain, but it also provides services basically similar to those of New York for very large portions of the earth's surface, particularly for the Sterling bloc. The Sterling bloc is the large number of nations that keep monetary accounts in pound sterling. Moscow is not only the preeminent service center of the U.S.S.R., a very large economic system in itself, but it also provides services basically similar to those of New York (though often under different names) for most of the rest of the Communist World, except such mavericks as China, Yugoslavia, and Albania.

The European Economic Community is a relatively new creation, though trends toward unifying the economic geography of Western Europe have been developing since the beginning of the Second Agglomerative Revolution. So far, no single center has emerged for that economic complex, but Paris seems to be attracting many functions similar to New York, London, and Moscow. For example, many European corporations (and subsidiaries of American firms) are locating their headquarters offices in Paris. Paris is already an important supranational service center, with a service hinterland that has extended well beyond France for a long time. It may well become the top supranational service center in the European Economic Community, if it is not already.

In the service hierarchy, the next level below the supranational service center is occupied by the national service centers, or for very large economic systems such as that of the United States, by major sub-national service centers such as Chicago. Such centers have lesser ranges than the supranational centers such as New York. Consequently, though the level and variety of services provided are truly impressive, they are distinctly of a lower hierarchical level. Only nations with relatively large, developed economies have such national service centers. For example, a developed but relatively small country such as Norway does not have a large enough economy so that Oslo can meet the necessary thresholds for many of these services. Consequently, Norway is included in the service hinterlands of service centers in other countries, particularly Stockholm and London. A very large underdeveloped country such as China has such a national service center (Peking or Shanghai), but generally the underdeveloped countries are too small in population and volume of economic activity to reach the necessary thresholds. Consequently, many of the higher-level services are not provided at all in them, or, if they are, they are provided by a service center in a larger and more developed country. In very large economic systems, such as the United States or the U.S.S.R., there may be major sub-national centers such as Chicago or Leningrad that provide services at levels similar to those of the national service centers of lesser economic systems. Often, national service centers are coincident with the national political capital, but not always. For example, Rome is the political and religious capital of Italy, but Milan is the preeminent service center.

A step below in the service hierarchy are such sub-national service centers as Cleveland, St. Louis, and Atlanta. Such centers have considerable ranges and relatively high levels of services, but distinctly of a lower order than those of New

York or Chicago. Perhaps the best single example of their level of services is their role as sub-national centers in the Federal Reserve Banking System of the United States.

The "lesser sub-national" service centers such as Pittsburgh, Cincinnati, and Seattle are just a step below the sub-national service centers. All of these are large in population and all provide relatively high levels of services. Yet if one uses banking as an index, they are subsidiary to the sub-national centers. For example, both Cincinnati and Pittsburgh are important centers in the Federal Reserve System, but subsidiary to Cleveland. The reader of this book is free to argue with my use of banking as an index. For example, if a concentration of corporate headquarters functions were used as the key index, then loyal Cincinnatians could rightly claim a higher place for Cincinnati in the hierarchy.

Still further down in the service hierarchy are all of the other metropolitan areas, many of them considerably smaller in population than the hypothetical metropolis of about one million population discussed in Chapter 3. Perhaps Dayton, Ohio, is a good example. Some of them are relatively large in *population*, and yet they do not occupy a very high place in the overall service network of the country. Sometimes this is because they are relatively new as metropolitan areas (though they may have existed as smaller places for a long time); it takes time to develop the expertise involved in the higher levels of services. Sometimes it is because they are too close to a center with an already developed high level of services. For example, Philadelphia is much more overshadowed by New York than it would be if it were located farther away. Despite this, the large population of Philadelphia and its very populous hinterland make Philadelphia one of our sub-national service centers. The same principle of overshadowing by a highly developed neighbor also operates at lower levels in the hierarchy, as with the regional metropolitan centers.

Broadly speaking, one can say that the geographic pattern of services *among* metropolitan areas resembles that of metropolitan hinterlands or that within metropolitan areas themselves. Certainly, the same principles of range, threshold, and hierarchy seem to apply. However, some differences are worth

Service Geography Beyond the Metropolis / 121

noting. At the lower levels of the service hierarchy it is useful to think of the usual or average shape of the hinterland of a service center as tending to be circular or hexagonal or perhaps oval in shape. When all of the special circumstances in specific cases are considered, these seem to be the most usual shapes for all of the thousands of hinterlands involved. But though no doubt this same tendency in the shape of the hinterland also applies at the upper levels of the service hierarchy, it is not a very useful guide to reality. There are too few cases and it is much more important to examine the exact shape of the hinterland with care if one wants to understand the center involved.

Similarly, political factors play a much more important role in determining the shape of the hinterland, and even its size, at the upper levels of the hierarchy. The higher the level of services, the more likely they are to be politically regulated. This is obvious in the case of such services as banking, insurance, and stock exchanging. But in many cases it also applies in such cultural services as music, the theater, and publishing. Many nations try to extend the range of their principal service center (often their capital) by subsidizing particular arts. The range for such subsidized services may well be much greater than for other, nonsubsidized, services. Of course, the notion of hinterlands as tending to be circular or oval in shape is of some value in helping to pinpoint such political influences on hinterland boundaries.

Change is important in the service geography of nations and of the whole earth, just as it is within the metropolis or in the metropolitan hinterland. Within the metropolis, there seems to be some modification of the historic Central Place pattern, particularly through the development of alternative service groupings: ribbon developments, arterial nodal developments, and specialized functional areas such as medical complexes.

Are any of these tendencies apparent at the national and international level? It seems so, particularly in the case of specialized functional areas. Megalopolis, that great urbanized strip of the United States Atlantic Seaboard extending from New Hampshire to Virginia, has had an unusually rapid development of national services in the last half century. Such higher-order national services include major universities, research centers, foundations, national publishers, communications specialists, and the chief policy makers of business, labor, and government. In short, Megalopolis is the principal home of the "Establishment" in the United States. The advantages of such a concentration are similar to those for a medical complex within a metropolis. That is, such a concentration helps communication among the service workers involved. The efforts of all of them are more effective because they can be in close touch with each other, often face-to-face. The disadvantage of such a geographic patterning is likewise similar to the disadvantage of the medical complex in a metropolis. That is, it increases the difficulty of those being served in making appropriate contacts with the service personnel. Perhaps some of the current criticism of the Establishment in the United States is based on a nostalgia for the simpler historic Central Place patterns in services. Perhaps some people sense that the older patterns are being eroded and are resisting this erosion.

Locational change at the level of nations or the whole earth is different from that at the metropolitan or metropolitan hinterland level in one very important respect. That is in terms of the information required to understand it. The people living in a metropolis may not fully comprehend all of the changes going on in the service pattern, but they can observe many of the shifts going on rather directly. Not so at the national and international level. Even if one travels a great deal around the earth, one is unlikely to develop a grasp of the overall service pattern and changes in it from direct observation alone. The areas involved are too great, the patterns too complex, and the forces producing the changes operate over too great a distance.

Instead, at this level, for even the most general understanding of the pattern, one must rely on secondhand or thirdhand information, on maps, census reports, and similar sources of current data, and on detailed interpretations by research workers. Consequently, changes in service geography at the upper levels may be very poorly understood by the inhabitants

Service Geography Beyond the Metropolis / 123

involved. Yet it seems apparent that the basic forces producing changes in the pattern (for example, population shifts, changes in transportation flows, and so forth) are basically similar at the metropolitan scale and at the international scale.

Just as there is resistance to locational change at the metropolitan level, there is resistance to locational change at the national and international level. And, similarly, this resistance is often rooted in the mental maps of the inhabitants. The service geography of a country at any particular point in time becomes a part of the culture, the mental outlook of the people. Partly, this is a matter of what is officially sanctioned and hence is taught in schools. But, more, it is passed on from one person to another through national communications media and by word of mouth. Thus, for Americans living today, it seems only right that Paris should be a supranational service center, particularly in the arts. Why? Because Parisians are currently doing an outstanding job in this type of service? Perhaps. Or perhaps more because everyone knows that Paris is "the city of light" and the "world art capital" (actually, New York currently is). Or, similarly, the established image of New York as the principal service center in America has enabled New York to hold its place despite other locational forces working against it (the southward and westward shift of the United States population, the elaboration of the United States transportation network, and so forth). Of course, the popular imagery about service geography does change over time; however it might lag behind reality. This is why it is difficult to predict changes in the hierarchy, especially at the upper levels of the service hierarchy.

Some Tentative Conclusions

It seems evident that the notion of Central Place Systems, including particularly the notions of range, threshold, and hierarchy, is the most useful general tool we now have for analyzing the service geography of the metropolis, its hinterland, and the linkages of metropolitan areas around the earth.

It seems also that the same process of selective thinning of the Central Place System as transportation and communication improve is now operating in all three kinds of areas. However, in the metropolis and its hinterland, there is a tendency toward the flattening of the historic Central Place hierarchy; but at the international level no flattening is as yet clearly evident. Instead, selective thinning seems to be working toward the advantage of the centers at the top of the hierarchy such as New York. Possibly this is because the flattening is occurring largely within the framework of developed economies, whereas the supranational centers serve both developed and underdeveloped areas. Possibly, as the whole earth becomes developed, that is, dominated by the notions inherent in the Second Agglomerative Revolution, the tendency toward a flattening of the Central Place System may become more general.

Within the metropolis, three alternative service patterns are emerging alongside the historic Central Place System: ribbon developments, nodal arterial patterns, and specialized functional areas. So far, only ribbon developments, or their counterparts, are clearly evident in metropolitan hinterlands, while it is the specialized functional areas (as represented by Megalopolis and its counterparts in Western Europe) which so far seem reflected at the national and international scale. Indeed, the metropolis is a mirror of service geography in general, though an imperfect mirror.

CHAPTER 8

Manufacturing Geography Beyond the Metropolis

To what degree is the location of manufacturing within nations and among nations analogous to the patterns within the metropolis? Are the great manufacturing regions of North America and Europe analogous to the industrial districts of the metropolis, and, if so, how? Are the same locational forces involved in both situations? Is the gradual spread of manufacturing away from the older manufacturing belts produced by the same forces luring manufacturing outward from the metropolitan core toward its periphery? Is industrial blight within parts of the metropolis essentially the same phenomenon as the plight of depressed areas such as Appalachia? Such questions are highly important if one wants to understand the locational pattern of a modern economy and to understand the sickness or health of the economy in various sections of a nation. But such questions cannot be answered at all in a book of this size without great simplification. To aid in such simplification, attention is focused on the American manufacturing pattern, within certain limits noted below.

Some Special Aspects of the American Pattern

How representative is the American manufacturing pattern? How well does it correspond to the general case in developed economies? First, it should be noted, the American economy has the largest volume of total production and the greatest variety or diversity in its production of any nation on earth. This has many implications for locational patterns. For example, specific *concentrations* of production can be larger as a result. Thus, the great size of the automobile complex of southeastern Michigan owes something to "Yankee ingenuity" without a doubt; but the total size of the United States economy has something to do with it too. Similarly, the greatest single metropolitan concentration of manufacturing on earth is in New York, but much of this is manufacturing for local consumption. This, in turn, is large in part because the top Central Place in an economy as large as that of the United States is bound to be large in its consuming population. All this implies that as other nations or groups of nations develop economic bases similarly large, they may also develop manufacturing concentrations similar to ours.

Second, the American economy is relatively self-contained. Though we are the largest single trading nation on earth, export-import trade is of minor dimensions in relation to internal trade. This means that, in the overall picture, most locational choices are made in a largely American context rather than in terms of linkages with overseas colonial areas and the like. This makes our manufacturing pattern easier to understand than the pattern of, say, Japan, whose manufacturing is much more dependent on overseas linkages. Historically, the manufacturing pattern of Europe has been more like that of Japan than that of the United States. That is, it has been heavily oriented to trade with non-European areas. But, now, with the development of greater European economic integration, a turning away from colonial interests, and the rise of mass-consumption patterns in Europe, European manufacturing patterns may well come to resemble ours more than they have. Specifically, this may well mean greater geographic concentration or agglomeration.

Third, greater economic freedom prevails in the United States than generally around the world. Though there are, indeed, political restrictions on locational choice in the United States, these are less significant than those in Western Europe or Japan and certainly much less significant than those in the Soviet Union. During the Stalinist era, the idea of security from military attack often dominated Soviet planning for the location of manufacturing. Thus the location of many factories in southern Siberia near mineral deposits was justifiable on military grounds, though hardly on the basis of nearness to markets, labor, industrial news, and the like. Contemporary locational planning in the U.S.S.R. gives these factors more weight in the locational equation, but political and military considerations remain more important than in the United States. In general, the American experience suggests what may emerge in Western Europe as the national frontiers lose their importance through economic union, and what might emerge in the Soviet Union if contemporary trends toward more flexibility in locational planning continue.

Fourth, the United States is larger in "effective national territory" than most nations. Canada, Brazil, and Australia are all relatively large; however, very large parts of their areas would be ruled out in locational decision-making today because of natural hazards and remoteness, so the locational choices for manufacturing are actually made within a much smaller geographic area than in the case of the United States. Both Japan and Western Europe have historically made their choices in manufacturing location within relatively cramped situations. Only the Soviet Union has had the opportunity to make locational choices within a great, expansive, and highly varied situation such as that of the United States. With this expansiveness the United States has had the opportunity to express a great variety of locational tendencies in various types of manufacturing. However, as Western Europe unifies economically, it, too, will have some of the same opportunities for locational experimentation.

Fifth, the American manufacturing pattern is of moderate age, so that it shows *some* of the effects of inertia—less than Europe but more than the newer manufacturing countries such as Canada, Australia, and the Soviet Union. Most of the discussion in subsequent pages stresses the kinds of factors important in making the initial choice of a factory site. But in reality, there is a great deal of inertia in manufacturing patterns. In a region having manufacturing now, there is very likely to be manufacturing in the future; not necessarily the same products, but manufacturing none the less. Hence, for a deep understanding of the manufacturing patterns of Europe, one must go beyond the contemporary scene to the distribution of population in the Middle Ages, to the Roman road pattern, to the location of medieval fairs, and so on. Similarly, the manufacturing pattern of the United States cannot be understood in depth without looking into the routes of westward migration, the effects of the post-Civil War freight rate patterns, and so on. As the newer manufacturing countries, such as Australia, age, their locational legacies will become more important.

Sixth, and finally, the American manufacturing economy is more advanced than that of most nations, more advanced even than those of Western Europe. This implies many things that affect locational choice. For example, automobiles, trucks, and pipe lines are a more important part of the overall transport system, with obvious effects on manufacturing locational choices. Similarly, in an advanced economy the location of raw materials from forest, field, and mine is less crucial in manufacturing choice than it is in a nation just beginning to build its manufacturing system. But the location of raw materials *from other manufacturers* is much more important than in an economy that is just beginning its development. Thus, industrial complexes such as those within the metropolis flourish over wide regions in an advanced economy.

In an advanced economy, the standard of living is high and this makes the pull of market attractions relatively more important than in less advanced economies. And, as the standard of living rises, there may be shifts in the manufactured products desired, with resulting effects on the locational pattern. For example, the manufacture and distribution of pleasure boats is a rather different enterprise from making ships or boats for fishing and commercial transportation. The more advanced the economy, the more important the roles of mass production and automation and hence the less the pull of low-wage labor. The more advanced the economy, the greater the role of services in the economy in general and in manufacturing itself; in an advanced economy the geography of manufacturing may be more closely linked with the service pattern than the pattern of producing primary products. An advanced economy implies a great development of managerial skills, with large bureaucratic organizations devoted to planning for manufacturing; in such economies, the role of face-to-face discussion among small producers is much reduced.

But with all of the differences that can be noted between the locational forces affecting manufacturing in the United States and other countries, the actual distribution of manufacturing in developed nations shows striking similarities to the American pattern. At this point, the reader might do well to verify this bold assertion by checking it against the data shown on the maps of a good set of economic atlases, such as those produced by the Oxford University Press. Apparently, some of the differences tend to cancel each other out. In any case, the similarities between the American pattern and the general pattern of developed countries are much more significant than the differences. Furthermore, it seems clear that the pattern in the United States often suggests what will develop in such countries as their economies mature and elaborate.

The Metropolis as a Manufacturing Mirror

The discussion in the following pages is closely linked with that in Chapter 4, because, to some degree, the manufacturing pattern of the metropolis is a mirror of American manufacturing patterns generally. However, it should be noted that it cannot be a perfect mirror because the transport system is rather different. The truck is particularly economical for relatively short hauls, as within a metropolis or its hinterland. Some other forms of transport (for example, railroads, large ships, and pipe lines) are particularly economical for long hauls, as for national linkages or interregional linkages. Therefore, though all forms of modern transportation are used within the metropolis as well as outside it, the effective mix, the overall transport system, is rather different in small areas such as the metropolis and in large areas such as the United States. This has profound effects on the kinds of locational choices made.

Likewise, even when the various accessibility costs and site costs being considered at the national scale are identical with those being considered at the metropolitan scale, there is no reason to assume that the relative weight that must be given to each of these factors will be the same. For example, though geographic variations in levels of taxation are certainly important in both cases, taxation must be given much greater weight in the locational equation within metropolitan areas than it is nationally because geographic differences in taxation are sharper.

Furthermore, even when the same factor is considered important in both cases, there is no reason to assume that this factor operates in the *same direction*. For example, attraction toward low-wage labor tends to pull manufacturing toward the core of the metropolis. But nationally, this same pull tends to disperse manufacturing away from developed areas toward rural areas.

Accessibility Costs: Raw Materials

The distribution of raw material sources within the United States is infinitely more complex than within the metropolis. In the metropolis, the main raw material sites are the transport terminals, the warehouses, and other factories. Nationally, these are also part of the picture, because sales from these points are seldom limited to the metropolis itself. And, of course, nationally, there are many metropolitan areas to be considered. But, in addition to this, there are an almost infinite number of widely dispersed farms, forests, and mines producing raw materials. Thus, saying that a manufacturer is attracted toward raw materials may mean a tendency toward dispersion (toward farming or forestry locations) or it may mean, conversely, an attraction toward a major transport node at the national level, such as Chicago.

Great loss of weight or bulk occurs in processing some raw

materials, but not others. Naturally, it is for the former that raw material locations are especially attractive as factory sites. For example, wood is often processed in forest regions or on the side of the forest region nearest the main markets. Similarly, the smelting or initial refining of many minerals (for example, copper, lead, zinc) often occurs in dispersed mining locations, far from the manufacturers of copper pots and pans or lead batteries, and far from the ultimate consumers of those products. Similarly, cotton ginning (removing of seeds from the fiber) usually occurs near the cotton fields; yet the weaving of cotton cloth is not necessarily found near raw cotton production because the weight loss in further processing is so much less significant. Attraction toward raw materials sometimes involves a perishability problem, too. For example, fruits and vegetables are often canned or frozen in factories near the fields.

In certain cases, attempts to reduce the transport costs of raw materials, combined with considerations of economies-of-scale in plant design, may produce manufacturing patterns analogous in some respects to the Central Place patterns of the geography of services (see Chapter 7). The distribution of butter and cheese factories in a dairy region such as Minnesota or Wisconsin is a good example. It is important to have the production of butter or cheese *near* the source of raw material (the dairy farms) both because of perishability and because of great weight loss in processing. Yet, on the other hand, there are important economies-of-scale achievable by increasing the size of the plant. However, since the production of milk is dispersed over wide areas of dairy farms, increasing the size of the plant beyond certain levels begins to greatly increase the transport costs involved in collecting the milk.

The result is a geographic compromise; the plants tend to be of moderate size, much larger than they would be if the butter and cheese were made on each and every dairy farm, yet much smaller than they would be if the processing were done only at major transport junctions such as Minneapolis, La Crosse, or Milwaukee. Since dairy farming is widely and relatively uniformly distributed over large areas, the source areas for the milk tend to be of comparable size and the plants tend to be of comparable size. In short, the concepts of threshold and range seem to apply here, though range in this case refers to sources of raw materials rather than sources of customers for a retailing outlet. However, the concept of hierarchy does not apply, because this production is specialized rather than involving a great variety of levels of products and services as in service geography.

Of course, attraction toward raw materials is often less simplistic than the examples cited thus far. Just as in the metropolis, there are many forms of manufacturing that involve the processing or assembling of *several* raw materials coming from a diversity of locations. And, just as in the metropolis, the location chosen for the manufacturing plant may not be at any one of those sites, but rather at a geometric compromise among them. For example, the iron and steel factories of Gary, Indiana, have few of the necessary raw materials available locally except such widely available materials as air, water, and sand. But Gary is located on the lakefront at a favorable transport node among iron ore sources (Minnesota and Quebec), limestone sources (especially the shores of the Great Lakes), and coal sources (Appalachia and southern Illinois).

Similarly, the industrial complexes discussed for the metropolis in Chapter 4 have counterparts on a broader geographic basis. Some are relatively small, linking a handful of cities and towns in a region. Others are very large, covering significant proportions of the nation. Examples of chemical complexes include the petrochemical complexes of the Gulf Coast (Texas-Louisiana) and the lower Delaware Valley, and the somewhat different chemical complexes of northeastern Ohio and the Kanawha Valley of West Virginia. Perhaps the best example of an assembly complex is the auto complex of southeastern Michigan, northern Indiana, and northwestern Ohio. Auto *parts* are produced in many, many plants in many different towns and cities. But the *assembly* of these occurs in a relatively few plants at key points in the region. As noted in Chapter 4, such linkages may be considered either as raw material attraction or as market attraction, depending on the point of view. For the assembly plant, the parts plants are sources of raw material. For the parts plants, the assembly plant is a market. But such problems in semantics should not obscure the basic reality: the importance of such industrial complexes in the manufacturing geography of advanced economies.

Perhaps the best single example of such an industrial complex on the national scale is the Iron-Steel Complex of the historic old "Manufacturing Belt." This belt, which has dominated all manufacturing in the United States since the late nineteenth century, extends from the Atlantic Ocean to approximately the Mississippi River and from approximately the Ohio River to the southern margins of the Great Lakes. Within this belt, there are several great concentrations of iron and steel production, notably in the Chicago area (especially in Gary, Indiana), the cities fringing Lake Erie (from Detroit to Buffalo), the lower Delaware and Susquehanna valleys, and the Pittsburgh-Wheeling area. These are locationally linked to sources of raw materials for the blast furnaces (especially coal, limestone, and iron ore, as noted previously for Gary) and more diverse sources of raw materials for the steel furnaces; but they are also locationally linked to the steel markets. These include particularly makers of railway equipment (Erie and Chicago), makers of auto parts (southeastern Michigan), ship builders (coastal cities from Boston to Norfolk), makers of farm machinery and earth-moving equipment (Illinois and Wisconsin), makers of machine tools (Cleveland and Cincinnati), builders of bridges and skyscrapers (especially in and around the various metropolitan areas of the belt), and a variety of other manufacturers of steel products (scattered throughout the belt).

If the reader plots these locations on a map of the United States he will begin to grasp the significance of industrial complexes in the manufacturing geography of the United States. Try it. Of course, for such manufacturers, the iron-steel producers are sources of raw materials; the markets for the producers of autos, and so on, are the consuming population of the United States at large, which is particularly concentrated in the metropolitan areas of this same manufacturing belt, or still other producers, many of whom are also located in the belt. As the steel products such as autos are worn out, they may be used for scrap, as raw material sources for the steel furnaces. If so, the main collecting points for the scrap are, of course, in the metropolitan areas scattered throughout the United States, but particularly in the Manufacturing Belt.

In short, in many respects the Iron-Steel Complex, like other industrial complexes, is a self-reinforcing geographic system. Specific details in such a locational system are of course subject to change, but the overall complex has great geographic permanence. Yet that does not necessarily make it all-enduring. As other metals challenge steel as the principal metal used in our society, this geographic pattern could be shaken to its foundations, particularly if the challenger, such as aluminum, had somewhat different locational requirements. Similarly, changes in the technology of steelmaking, with effects on the proportions of various raw materials used and the uses to which steel could be put, might ultimately require major readjustments in such a geographic pattern. However, changes in the details of a geographic pattern can occur without basically changing the major outlines of the pattern. We are accustomed to thinking of agricultural patterns, and patterns of the land generally, as being all-enduring and almost everlasting; yet it may be that the geographic framework of industrial complexes will endure far longer than specific contemporary agricultural patterns (see Chapter 9).

The emergence of such industrial complexes is one of the more significant factors retarding the spread of manufacturing away from established manufacturing regions, either within a nation or among nations. That is, the locational handicap of a state such as Arkansas in trying to attract industry is basically similar to the handicap of an underdeveloped country such as Ghana in trying to attract industry. Other things being equal, it is often cheaper to locate with respect to an established industrial complex than it is to seek out more distant sites. However, not all manufacturing located in the Manufacturing Belt is so closely linked with the

Iron-Steel Complex that it cannot move. For example, the textile industry is linked only peripherally with the Iron-Steel Complex through the steel machinery used. So that can move more readily from a location in the Manufacturing Belt to the Southeast. Similarly, garment making has some links to the complex, but not strong ones, so garment making is more free to leave the belt. As is furniture making (wood furniture), moving toward the Southeast, or the aerospace industry to the Gulf and the West Coast, and so on.

And if the overall attraction of industries (and hence population) to these peripheral areas is great enough, the market for steel products in such areas may become great enough to offset the disadvantages of locating steel product plants away from the established Iron-Steel Complex. Hence the manufacturing of various products from steel in modest-sized plants may emerge in those market areas, and, if enough of this develops, steel manufacturing itself in modest-sized concentrations may also emerge. This has happened in the United States, so that there are now various outlying geographic extensions of the basic Iron-Steel Complex of the Northeast and Middle West. The same basic process or sequence seems to be involved in the spread of manufacturing away from the developed countries to the underdeveloped countries.

Accessibility Costs: Markets

Some aspects of the attraction toward markets have been discussed already in relation to industrial complexes. Other aspects are treated here. Some manufacturing processes involve a great gain in weight or bulk, for example, the bottling of soft drinks or the assembling of refrigerators, while others do not. Obviously it is for the former that closeness to market is most crucial. Just as with raw materials, the perishability problem is sometimes involved, for example, with ice cream or custard made from dry ingredients. This, too, increases the importance of nearness to market.

Range and threshold considerations are often important in interpreting the actual meaning of "attraction to market."

For example, bread making was once an almost ubiquitous industry. Every community over the size of a hamlet tended to have a bakery. Transportation was slow and expensive, so bakeries had to be close to customers and hence small. Economies-of-scale in production were very limited; bread making was essentially a handicraft operation. But then bread making became more mechanized and hence important economies-of-scale emerged. But the range of a bakery was still quite restricted except in areas of very dense population, as in a major metropolitan area. So bread making remained generally ubiquitous, though bakeries became large in major metropolitan areas. Then, improvements in transportation, most particularly the truck and the interstate highway system, changed the practical meaning of range.

Today, more and more, large *regional* bakeries are emerging, producing for the metropolitan hinterland as well as the metropolis itself. Or, even, producing for several adjacent metropolitan areas and their hinterlands. Bread baking is really not a ubiquitous industry any more. Perhaps the congressman who sought to promote United States manufacturing by suggesting that Marshall Plan wheat be milled and baked in the United States was not as fatuous as he sounded. Maybe he was just ahead of his time!

The evolution of the auto industry also illustrates how the practical meaning of attraction to market can change over time. Assembled, bulky items such as autos often tend to be produced near their market because it is cheaper to ship the unassembled parts than it is to ship the bulky final product. Yet, on the other hand, there are very significant economies-of-scale possible if very large assembly plants are built. Before the days of Henry Ford, the auto industry was small in overall volume of production and was dispersed in a large number of very small plants in various parts of the nation. Henry Ford and his associates showed that the economies-of-scale in very large assembly-line operations were more than enough to offset the increased costs from locating far from most customers. Hence the industry became highly concentrated in southeastern Michigan and environs.

However, as the overall volume of business grew and grew

Manufacturing Geography Beyond the Metropolis / 137

and the population of the United States became more and more concentrated in metropolitan areas and megalopolitan zones, it finally became possible to achieve *both* economies-of-scale in plant operation and a reduction in costs of transporting finished autos to customers. After World War II, quite a number of *regional* auto assembly plants were established in various parts of the nation to supplement the main Michigan concentration. Each was large enough to achieve the necessary economies-of-scale and was near potential customers. Changes in the technology of auto construction, or changes in the nature of assembly-line operations, or changes in the distribution of the consuming population may make some new geographic pattern more practical in the auto industry at some time in the future. Attraction to market is not a static concept.

This same dilemma of threshold and range considerations is very useful in interpreting changes in the location of many other kinds of manufacturing in a metropolitan economy such as that of the United States. By the late nineteenth and early twentieth centuries, Metropolitan New York had become not only the largest single manufacturing metropolis in the United States, containing about 10 percent of all United States manufacturing, but also it was by far the most *diversified*. It was easier to list the things *not* manufactured in New York than to list what *was* manufactured there. Some of this production was largely for national markets (for example, clothing, jewelry, and toys), but the great diversity in production reflected primarily the market attraction of the very large population of New York itself. For a long time, New York manufacturing was much more diversified than that of metropolitan areas generally.

But in recent decades, there has been a widespread tendency for the manufacturing of the larger metropolitan areas to become more and more diversified. Why? The best explanation seems to involve the threshold-range dilemma. As the metropolitan areas grow in population and as transport linkages with hinterlands improve, more and more manufacturing thresholds are being reached and hence the attraction to market can be expressed by the rise of new forms of manufacturing in these metropolitan areas without their incurring ruinous "diseconomies-of-scale." New York is still the largest and most diversified, but it is losing some of its special advantages related to size. On a national scale, this means a flattening of the Manufacturing Map.

Accessibility Costs: Labor

Accessibility to labor may mean either accessibility to low-wage labor or it may mean accessibility to labor with special skills or attitudes. The attraction of low-wage labor has long been one of the principal factors luring industry away from established metropolitan areas toward more dispersed locations in the hinterland of the metropolis or toward less developed areas. Naturally, this has been most significant for those forms of manufacturing in which labor costs are a major part of all manufacturing costs. Examples include cotton textiles, the more routine types of garment making, and many kinds of agricultural processing. But for a highly automated industry such as petroleum refining, the attraction of low-wage labor has been a very minor locational factor.

Geographic variations in wages are much greater at the national scale than they are within a single metropolis; hence, this factor has been much more important at the national level than within the metropolis (see Chapter 4). No doubt it will always be more important nationally than in areas of greater uniformity, such as a metropolis. However, all major trends in the Second Agglomerative Revolution suggest that this locational factor is of declining importance. The pool of surplus rural labor associated with the transformation of agriculture (see Chapter 9) will gradually dry up, no doubt. Similarly, equalization of educational opportunity will reduce differences in the mobility of workers and potential workers in different geographic settings. Likewise, nationwide industrial bargaining and nationwide welfare legislation (such as Social Security) will reduce geographic variations. In short, this factor is highly significant today, but may not be for long.

At one time, industrial skills were primarily learned on the job and passed on from father to son. So industry was loath to leave the areas in which it was already established. For example, the skills needed in tailoring or in the machine tool industry were simply not available everywhere and workers with such skills were often unwilling to move. This is still an important stabilizing force in the geographic pattern of manufacturing and probably always will be to some extent. Yet as more and more industries become more and more highly automated, the most crucial skills are those of the engineer rather than the craftsman. And engineers, like others with a relatively high level of education, are much more willing to move to new localities than were their craftsmen forebears. Thus, the attraction of the new locality can become crucial: places with social, recreational, or educational advantages (particularly metropolitan areas), places with attractive climates (especially the West, Southwest, and parts of the Southeast), or places with less urban blight than the older manufacturing areas (especially the metropolitan hinterlands in the North and the newer urban areas in the South and West).

Accessibility Costs: Services

At the national level, geographic variations in the availability of services are a much more important locational factor than they are within the metropolis. The level of services available to assist manufacturing, including both governmentally provided services and business services-for-hire, is lowest in the least densely populated and the poorest rural areas. There, such services are minimal, usually below the threshold for any but the simplest forms of manufacturing. From such areas, the level of manufacturing services gradually rises through the hinterlands of the metropolitan areas and is the highest in the metropolitan areas themselves. Among the metropolitan areas, the levels also vary. They are the most complete and the most diversified in major metropolitan areas such as New York. The availability of such services in a particular area is most important for the small firm, particularly the new, small firm; a large, national manufacturing firm is much more able to provide such services for itself or to ensure their development with minimal difficulty.

Historically, services have tended to be a conservative locational force, stabilizing the location of manufacturing rather than encouraging its dispersal. Naturally, business services-for-hire tend to grow up in places already having a demand for them; once in existence, they tend to favor such places over new places without such an accretion of services. Similarly, governmentally provided services require a tax base to support them. An area already having manufacturing has a better tax base with which to provide services than a less developed area does.

However, there can be downward spirals of service clusters just as there can be upward spirals of service clusters. A declining industrial area may attempt to improve its services to lure replacement industry, but if the level of taxation rises to do this, the area may become unattractive because of its tax patterns. Older manufacturing areas, particularly the older metropolitan areas, often bear an unequal share of the welfare burden; they often have a higher percentage of the elderly and the poor concentrated in them. In attempting to meet this welfare burden, the level of services directly related to manufacturing may decline, thus favoring the movement of industry away from them. For the new manufacturing areas, the trick is to get an upward spiral in services started; for older areas, the trick is to maintain their advantage and to halt any trends toward the development of a downward spiral.

Of course, the new, small firm can grow up into a national giant, thus changing its service needs. For example, the service complex of New York was important for the struggling radio industry in its infancy. But, later, the great electronics firms were less tied to major established service clusters and the industry became more geographically dispersed. Similarly, insofar as services are provided by the national government rather than by local governments, the advantage of the established metropolitan area or hinterland locality is reduced.

Providing electrical power is a somewhat special case because very large quantities of cheap electrical power are particularly needed by certain industries such as aluminum refining. At one time, aluminum refining tended to be attracted to major hydroelectric sites because of such abundant, cheap power. Later, electrical production sites using natural gas were better able to meet this need, so new refining plants were located in quite different parts of the United States. Still later, sites accessible to coal became more prominent, and new geographic patterns in aluminum refining emerged. As a result, aluminum refining today in the United States is found in large plants at all three kinds of sites and consequently is quite widely dispersed.

Actually, threshold and range considerations in the production of electrical power were very much involved. Economies-of-scale are very important in power production. A power company could choose to sell the power from a new facility over a wide geographic area, incurring considerable distribution costs in so doing and having to wait for the gradual increase in the level of power consumption in that region. Or, the company could sell a large proportion of the power to a single customer, such as an aluminum refining plant, which could locate close to the power plant, and would take large quantities of power as soon as the plant opened. Because of the great economic advantages of the latter choice, the power producer has often been willing to make substantial price concessions to the aluminum refiner to attract him. Such considerations are obviously less significant in established manufacturing areas, with their large and diversified consumption of power, than in areas with little established manufacturing. In short, threshold and range considerations related to power production have sometimes encouraged the dispersal of industry away from established centers toward the less developed zones.

Accessibility Costs: Business News and Gossip

On the national level, this factor is of minimal importance for the location of manufacturing, even though it is of considerable importance within metropolitan areas. Nationally, this problem of accessibility is largely solved by geographically separating the different levels of manufacturing management. In the large, national firm the central management function is carried on particularly in the chief centers of business news and gossip, the leading metropolitan areas; the more routine management functions can be carried on elsewhere and so branch plants can be built in many places remote from such news, in the hinterlands as well as in the lesser metropolitan areas. The larger the manufacturing firm, the greater its separation into many plants; the greater the geographic scope of the firm, the more the headquarters office is likely to be found in a major metropolitan area such as New York or Chicago, and the more likely the individual plants are to be located with respect to other locational considerations.

Site Costs

The transport costs involved in getting materials or labor to and from the manufacturing site (accessibility costs) are only one side of the locational problem. The other side involves costs incurred at the site itself, such as taxes, land costs, building costs, and so on. Building costs vary more nationally than they do within metropolitan areas, particularly because of climatic variations. For example, in warm, dry areas such as the Southwest, some industries such as the air frame industry can be carried on at least partially out of doors, thus reducing building costs. But, on the national level geographic variations in land costs and in taxes are generally not as sharp as these variations are within metropolitan areas. Hence these factors are less important nationally in determining the manufacturing pattern than they are within metropolitan areas.

Government Regulation of Manufacturing Location

Within metropolitan areas, zoning laws establish specific geographic frames of reference within which manufacturing must locate. On the national level in the United States, there is nothing comparable to such metropolitan zoning laws. In Great Britain and some other industrialized nations, there is considerable national regulation of manufacturing location, but not in the United States. Of course, manufacturing is excluded from certain national areas such as national parks, but this is minimal in overall importance. Also, from time to time the national government has sought, through various subsidies, to encourage manufacturing to disperse away from established metropolitan areas and to locate in depressed economic areas such as Appalachia. However, the indirect effects of governmental purchases and governmental decisions on the location of defense establishments and research centers probably affect the national Manufacturing Map much more than any specific locational program such as that for Appalachia. Similarly, federal taxation policies, particularly those involving the rapid amortization of buildings and equipment, generally encourage locational response to changing factors affecting location, but they do not specify just where manufacturing can or cannot locate, as do local zoning laws.

At the level of state governments, there has been the famous contemporary "war between the states" whereby various states try to lure industry away from each other through various subsidies and tax concessions. However, attracting industry in this fashion is not very effective in the long run unless the site within the state has basic advantages in its mix of accessibility costs and site costs. Of course, if two sites in different states were of nearly equal advantage in all other factors, then the existence of a locational subsidy in one state and not the other might be crucial in the ultimate locational choice. In general, zoning laws are used in a relatively negative way within metropolitan areas, to *exclude* manufacturing from certain areas; on the state and national levels, governmental efforts at influencing location are more often of a positive nature, involving attempts to *attract* industry to particular places.

The Resolution of Locational Choice at the National Level

It is the *balance* among the various locational costs that the manufacturer must consider, not just one alone. And, of course, different forms of manufacturing incur different proportions of the various locational costs. But, in general, accessibility costs are much more important than site costs at the national level. The basic choice of an area is likely to be made primarily on the basis of accessibility costs, particularly for raw materials, markets, and services. Once a general area has been chosen, site costs and the other accessibility factors are likely to play a role in the selection of the specific site within that area.

Some locational factors tend to encourage industry to concentrate rather than to disperse. The concentration may be in major metropolitan areas or clusterings of such metropolitan areas into megalopolitan zones. Or, it may be a somewhat looser form of concentration, as in broad industrial complexes such as the Iron-Steel Complex of the old Manufacturing Belt. Factors favoring such concentration include population concentration (concentration of markets), transport nodalities (making raw materials cheaply available), hierarchies in service geography (see Chapter 7), and the raw material market interdependencies of industrial complexes.

But other locational factors tend to encourage manufacturing to disperse more widely, either into the small towns of the hinterland of a manufacturing metropolis or into more distant areas with little or no previous manufacturing. Such factors include the attraction of manufacturing toward dispersed primary production sites, attraction toward widely dispersed markets (the population of farming areas), attraction toward widely dispersed low-wage labor (farmers underemployed by the mechanization of agriculture), attraction toward dispersed sources of cheap power (a hydroelectric plant in a remote location), and most site costs.

Some locational factors tend toward industrial inertia, toward retaining manufacturing in the areas in which it is already established and retarding its movement away from these to areas without manufacturing. Examples include the roles of service clusters, fixed investments in buildings and nonmovable equipment, established concentrations of markets, concentrations of skilled labor, low-wage labor concentrated in metropolitan slums, and the like. In addition, the mental maps of locational decision-makers are generally weighted in favor of established areas. "Follow the leader" tendencies among locational decision-makers may either support the established pattern or assist in creating new ones, depending on the circumstances. Perhaps the role of major national firms in bringing manufacturing to untried territory is basically similar to the role of major retailers in ensuring the success of new suburban shopping centers. Where the "big ones" go, there must be potential, some argue, so the smaller ones are more likely to follow to the same or similar areas. Contrarily, if the big ones stay put, then perhaps that is wise, some argue.

Yet other locational factors tend to break established geographic patterns for manufacturing. These include the tendency for some primary production sites, such as those for some types of mining, to shift radically in relatively short periods. They also include the possibility of escaping onerous burdens in the established manufacturing areas, such as unfavorable labor relations, heavy taxation to support accumulated indigents (the elderly or the unemployable), and outmoded buildings or equipment. Likewise, they include the development of new forms of manufacturing that are freer to create new geographic patterns than older forms of manufacturing, for example, the movie industry in the 1920s or the aerospace industry today. And, of course, changes in the transport network or in service geography encourage new geographic patterns in manufacturing.

Interpreting the Manufacturing Map of the United States

The net effect of all the locational tendencies and countertendencies for manufacturing discussed in this chapter is to create an extraordinarily diverse and very dynamic pattern. If the reader has not already done so, he should at this point open a good economic atlas such as the *Oxford Economic Atlas of the United States and Canada*. He should check actual manufacturing distributions against the broad generalizations discussed here to see if he can find any exceptions to the word picture I have painted (yes, there are some!). Likewise, he should examine each economic map to see how, on the contemporary scene, the relative significance of the various attractive forces might be working out for specific forms of manufacturing, for example, the paper industry. Though the overall pattern shows a very strong attraction toward raw materials, both toward commercial forestry regions and toward coastal sites at transport nodes favorably situated with reference to forest sources, there is also clear evidence of an attraction toward markets (especially the major metropolitan areas) and even toward highly specialized markets (such as book publishing or the printing of business forms). This is not a chore. It is a fascinating game of "who done it," a chance to have fun puzzling out, industry by industry, what the relative strengths of the various locational forces might be today.

If the reader wanted to pursue the matter further, it would be useful to look up maps showing similar patterns at an earlier date. For some industries, such study would show only relatively minor change, but for others there have been dramatic shifts in location in the last half century. It is fun to try to puzzle out just which ones and why. If the reader wished to pursue the matter still further, he would want to consult the United States Censuses of Manufacturing and some of the references in this book that show ways of approaching the manufacturing location problem in terms of mathematics and geometry.

Or, the reader could carry these generalizations forward by plotting various manufacturing regions such as the historic Manufacturing Belt on a map, along with subsidiary regions such as the Carolina-Georgia Piedmont, or the Texas-Gulf region, or the Los Angeles-San Diego complex, or subdivisions of larger regions such as the Manufacturing Belt. A broad concept such as the Manufacturing Belt really does not say very much. It is only when one gets into the subdivisions of that region, such as the Miami Valley of southwestern Ohio or the Connecticut Valley of New England, that one begins to bridge the gap between abstraction and reality. But, in any case, the derivation of such regional generalizations by the reader himself is essential if the geography of manufacturing is to come alive for him.

At this point, the reader may also wish to review Chapter 4, on manufacturing in the metropolis, in connection with this chapter, on manufacturing in developed economies in general. If my interpretations are correct, the metropolis is less faithful as a mirror of manufacturing distributions than as a mirror of service distributions (Chapters 3 and 7). Basically the same locational forces seem to operate, but the significance of the various forces differs dramatically in the two cases and the forces do not always operate in the same geographic directions. This is not to say that one does not find the Manufacturing Map of the metropolis reflected in the nation at large. Indeed one does. Manufacturing regions in the nation *are* broadly analogous to industrial districts in the metropolis; depressed areas such as Appalachia *are* broadly analogous to blighted industrial districts in the metropolis, handicapped by obsolescent buildings and other patterns; the industrial complexes of the metropolis *are* reflected in broadly similar geographic linkages at a wide variety of levels in various parts of the nation. Similarly, the roles of markets, raw materials, and services *are* important in both cases. And so on; there are many similarities.

Yet, on the other hand, there are important differences. The role of geographic wage differentials is dissimilar; the geographic separation of management functions modifies the meaning of linkages to the service network; variations in real estate taxes and land costs are less marked; the role of governmental regulation of location is quite different. And so on. There are numerous differences. Perhaps the most important one is that in the metropolis the outward shift of manufacturing to the suburban ring and beyond into the adjacent hinterland seems to be an inexorable tendency today. On the national scene, there is, of course, some tendency for manufacturing to disperse away from the regions in which it has been long established, but this tendency appears rather weaker than the tendency to disperse outward from the metropolis. And it does not as generally operate in *all directions*. The likelihood of an area without manufacturing attracting manufacturing is less at the national scale than in the periphery of the metropolis, or so it seems.

The general trend for manufacturing location in the United States seems to be toward more diffusion in the great megalopolitan zones and toward loose clusterings in the general vicinity of established metropolitan areas, rather than toward a general diffusion throughout the area of the United States. This has implications not only for the geography of manufacturing itself and for the geography of services, but also for the emerging patterns of primary production discussed in the following chapter.

CHAPTER 9

Primary Production Beyond the Fringes of the Metropolis

Primary production is often discussed as a world-wide phenomenon. And, indeed, agriculture is found in underdeveloped and developed economies alike. But the differences in the primary production in the two settings are more significant than the similarities. In underdeveloped economies, primary production, and especially agriculture, tends to be the locational framework around which all other locational decisions are made. But in developed economies such as that of the United States, agricultural locations are only part of the overall mix and only infrequently are they a controlling part of that mix. Hence, the primary production of underdeveloped countries is discussed separately in this book, in Chapter 11. Here, attention is focused on the agriculture, forestry, and mining of developed economies. Though each of these is discussed sequentially, there is a general concern throughout with how and why these patterns might be like or different from each other; and with how each might be like or different from what has been described in previous chapters for services and manufacturing. In short, the emphasis is on how primary production patterns mesh with other patterns in an advanced economy to produce contemporary economic geography.

I: AGRICULTURE

There is more confusion about the locational patterns of agriculture than about any other form of production. There is less willingness to accept factual evidence about changes now going on, less willingness to give up cherished images about the farmer and farming. This is not surprising. The very foundations of Western civilization are rooted in attitudes and ideas formed long ago. For ten thousand years the whole economy and the whole culture were immersed in a pervasive agricultural way of life. The Occidental value system has been related to a particular locational pattern for agriculture and, indeed, has been supportive of that pattern. We, who are inheritors of that tradition, can be forgiven, I think, if we cling to outmoded conceptions about the distribution of agriculture. It takes time for the fundamental rethinking of all things that has been made necessary by the Second Agglomerative Revolution.

Hence, the first step in "telling it like it is" for contemporary agriculture is to clear away some cobwebs by asking the reader to open a good modern economic atlas such as the *Oxford Economic Atlas of the United States and Canada*. Before reading further, the reader should study the agricultural maps with some care and ask himself some pointed questions about them. Why such-and-such a particular agricultural production pattern and not some other? What alternative rational explanations could there be for such patterns? What are their relative merits? How far do time-honored explanations about the "natural advantages" of particular soils or climates actually go in making sense of the maps? Or, for that matter, how far does the traditional "nearness to market" argument actually take us in unraveling the meaning of the maps? Or, to what degree do the maps seem to support our images of a simple, grandfatherly kind of farm (the kind described in the Dick-and-Jane books)? Clearly, if we are to understand the locational patterns of a modern economy we must develop somewhat more sophisticated interpretations, interpretations rivaling the sophistication of modern agriculture itself.

Our difficulties in unraveling such maps are not all our fault, not all rooted in our clinging to old ideas. Part of the difficulty is that the transformation of agriculture associated with the Second Agglomerative Revolution is still incomplete. That is, maps of agricultural production are a composite of two contrasting cultures, one basically urban-industrial and the other traditional and rural. Though most production comes from the "businesslike farmer," there is also some from the "way-of-life" farmer. The two differ primarily in attitude. Each is fulfilling a role. The way-of-life farmer thinks of himself as a farmer and does what he assumes farmers do; the businesslike farmer thinks of himself as a businessman primarily and a farmer only secondarily and he does what he assumes businessmen do. For example, he may be just as avid a bookkeeper as his urban counterpart, just as concerned with profit and loss accounting. He is likely to make clear distinctions between his job or vocation and his hobbies. The way-of-life farmer is more relaxed about it all. Usually, his hobbies and his vocaton fuse together. Indeed, he may have quite an aversion to bookkeeping because careful accounts might point up too glaringly just how much of this total time is spent on production activities that could only be justified as hobbies.

But though both cultures are indeed represented in the agricultural areas of advanced economies, it is farming as a business that increasingly shapes the overall geographic pattern of production. The businesslike farmer overwhelmingly outproduces the way-of-life farmer. The way-of-life farmers account for only a small and declining proportion of total production. They are attempting to perpetuate many of the old ways of life of our ancestors as best they can, producing farm products in small volume by antiquated methods at prices depressed by the more efficient, businesslike farmers. Such farming survivals from an earlier age would be more appropriately discussed as a part of a "geography of poverty" or a "geography of cultural survivals," or even as a "geography of underdeveloped areas" than as a part of the geography of primary production. In short, the rest of this discussion focuses on the locational patterns of businesslike farming because that is responsible for the main outlines of the contemporary pattern in advanced countries and will be even more so in the future.

Differences in Agricultural Location

How might one best go about trying to analyze the location of agricultural production by businesslike farmers? On the one hand, one might start by assuming that the problem of location for such a farmer is inherently different from that of a retailer or a manufacturer. For example, it has been said that the farmer starts with his site as a given and looks about for kinds of production that he might carry on at that site to make a profit, whereas presumably the manufacturer starts with some sort of decision about what to manufacture and then looks for an appropriate site at which to do it. If this is true for businesslike farmers generally, then perhaps the locational problem *is* different in a fundamental way.

On the other hand, one could start with the assumption that the similarities between the farmer's choices and those of his urban counterparts are much more important than the differences. In that case, perhaps some of the ideas about service geography or manufacturing geography discussed earlier in this book would be useful in interpreting agricultural patterns. If one is as impressed by the sweeping nature of the Second Agglomerative Revolution as I am, particularly by the tendency of metropolitan ideas to spread to even the most remote rural areas, then one is likely to opt for the latter position. But if one is more comfortable with more traditional approaches, then one would opt for the former and stress the *differences* between agricultural patterns and those of services or manufacturing.

Undeniably, there are differences in the locational problems. It is only whether or not these differences outweigh the similarities that is at issue. Traditionally, at last four differences are notable. One involves the question of *multiple products*. The farm of the past was usually a general farm producing many different products, rather than a specialized farm producing only one or a few. This was in sharp contrast to the retailer or manufacturer who specialized in only one product or class of products. But today many forms of manufacturing involve multiple products, too. For a really complex locational problem, try analyzing an oil refinery with its very complex mix of multiple products. Meanwhile, though some farmers continue to be general farmers with multiple products, others are highly specialized. No, the question of multiple products is not a basic difference for agricultural location.

Traditionally, the farmer's attitude toward *land ownership* has been different. The farmer tended to go into farming at or near the site at which he was born. From this site he looked about for the production mix that would be most profitable. The businesslike farmer of today sometimes does this, too. But it would be a grave mistake to assume that he is necessarily very sentimental about particular pieces of real estate. He is likely to be relatively well-educated, well-traveled, and socially mobile. He may be quite willing to buy and sell sites. Or to rent them. Often he is not an individual at all, but rather a corporation, with all the loss of sentimental attachments to specific pieces of real estate that that implies. In short, though the way-of-life farmer may think primarily in terms of *land,* the businesslike farmer is more likely to think in terms of *real estate,* and be flexible about location.

The traditional *organizational atomization* of agriculture is a more real difference for businesslike farming, though it is less significant than formerly. By organizational atomization, I mean the tendency to have thousands and thousands of producers rather than only a few. Agriculture notoriously involves a very large number of producing units. There were over six million farms in the United States in 1935. This contrasts sharply with the great concentration of the steel industry in a relatively few firms. Or the auto industry into the Big Three. And so on. But it is important to remember that the trend toward the concentration of production into a relatively few large organizations is a recent phenomenon, primarily a development of the last century. Nor is this trend complete in either services or manufacturing. Though we tend to think of General Electric or Ford or General Motors when we think of manufacturing, in fact many branches of manufacturing are still dominated by small firms. Garment making is an example. Toymaking is another. And though there are indeed giant department stores and department store chains, so also are there many small retail firms.

True, agriculture has lagged behind the general trend away from organizational atomization. Yet from 1935 to 1968 the number of farms in the United States decreased by about 50 percent. Meanwhile, the average acreage and investment per farm were increasing. The trend toward concentration is much faster in some types of agriculture than others, as might be expected. Agriculture as a whole is quite as much a mixed bag as is manufacturing as a whole. Currently, cattle feeding is becoming simultaneously concentrated geographically and organizationally. Although there were thousands of feed lots in the United States in the late-1960s, about one-fourth of all cattle feeding occurred on the 225 largest feed lots. These large lots had capacities of 8,000 or more head, a dramatic change from the past. No doubt various forms of modern technology, such as the computer, will make it easier and easier for agriculture to follow the general trend away from organizational atomization. However, in the short run, the pattern of even businesslike farming does differ in this way from some aspects of services and manufacturing.

Traditionally, it has been held that the *biological nature* of farm production somehow makes the locational problem quite different. Production must be geared to the life cycle of plants and animals, which varies widely from annual crops such as wheat (for which locational decisions can be made annually) to long-lived perennials such as olives. Yet the production cycle also varies widely in manufacturing, from the long lead time needed for military aircraft (several years) to the short lead time for women's dresses (days or weeks).

Hypothetically, the space requirements for farming are biological in origin. Traditionally, manufacturing occurs in a *point pattern*, using relatively little space for each factory, whereas agriculture occurs in an *area pattern*, spread out over great expanses of territory. But is this rooted in biology and hence relatively unchangeable or is it essentially an economic phenomenon? In the days of general farming, most animals were raised on crop farms and since crop production was spread out, animal farming was spread out, too. But in recent decades there is more and more tendency to separate animal rearing and crop producing geographically. This has permitted the rise of "egg factories" in New Jersey, "broiler factories" in Georgia, "dairy factories" in the Los Angeles area, "beef factories" in the Colorado Piedmont, "pork factories" in Iowa, and so on. In short, a trend toward geographic concentration or a point pattern for animal rearing is clearly evident.

The tendency for crop production to be spread out is, perhaps, more intractable. Crop production is a controlled form of photosynthesis, a conversion of one form of energy (usually sunlight) to another (edible foods, and so on). As long as sunlight is the principal energy source, then crop production must be spread out because sunlight is spread out. However, insofar as other energy sources can be substituted, the area requirement is broken. For example, mushroom production is highly concentrated (in the United States, near Philadelphia) and flowers and vegetables are sometimes raised under artificial (fluorescent) lights. Generally, crop production continues to be spread out because land and sunlight are relatively cheap in relation to alternative energy sources. If the cost of land (and hence sunlight) rises sufficiently in the future (as through land scarcities induced by population growth, demands for recreation space, and so on), then crop farming, too, will shift from an area pattern toward a point pattern.

Admittedly, such a shift appears a long way off and perhaps it will never occur. But the possibility of it underlines the fact that it is the energy source used for crop farming that is crucial in the present pattern, rather than immutable biological considerations. And it is worth remembering that as long as manufacturing depended on widely dispersed energy sources (human and animal muscle power, straw, charcoal, and so on), then it was very widely dispersed. But once a shift in energy sources occurred (to electricity, coal, petroleum, and so on) a much more concentrated pattern was possible. In short, for the immediately foreseeable future, the spread-out nature of crop farming will make it locationally different from manufacturing in some respects, but this is a function of the present state of our technology and hence may change as the Second Agglomerative Revolution rolls onward.

Similarities in Agricultural Location

Though some aspects of even businesslike farming continue to make the locational problem different, other aspects have combined to make the locational choices of the farmer essentially similar to those of the manufacturer. Hence the following discussion uses the *least-cost approach* previously used in Chapters 4 and 8 for manufacturing.

Accessibility Costs: Markets

As the consuming populations of developed countries have become more and more concentrated in metropolitan and megalopolitan zones, the question of distance to market has become more and more significant. In earlier times, economic geographers tended to ignore this question, even though a brilliant theoretical analysis of the relation of distance and markets was developed quite early by a nineteenth century economist and economic geographer, von Thunen. Today, in their enthusiasm over the rediscovery of the von Thunen model, some economic geographers are in danger of overstressing this single accessibility cost at the expense of other equally important accessibility costs.

The von Thunen theory is a *land-use* theory. That is, it purports to explain how the land around a market point will be used, either considering transport costs alone or making the analysis more complicated by including other variables (such as variations in soil fertility). In many respects it resembles the concept of a cone of decreasing land values away from the CBD of the metropolis (Chapters 4, 5, and 6). It stresses how land use might be affected by market competition for land, rather than stressing the attitudes of individuals making choices about location, a consistent theme in many parts of this book.

In its simplest form, the von Thunen theory states that, *other things being equal*, competition among farming land uses around a single market point will be directly related to distance from that market point. As a formula, it is that:

$$R \text{ equals } E(p-a) - Efk$$

when:

"R" means the net return to the principal factor of production, land,
"E" means output per acre,
"p" means market price per commodity unit,
"a" means production cost per unit of commodity,
"f" means transport rate per mile for unit of commodity, and
"k" means the distance to market in miles.

Such a formula assumes that there is a free market for land, without political interference in the form of acreage controls, subsidies, and the like. In such a free market, the highest bidders for land would have first choice, the next highest bidders would have the next choice, and so on.

How would agricultural production be locationally affected thereby? In two ways. First, farming would tend to be most intensive immediately adjacent to the market point and gradually decrease in intensity in all directions. In intensive agriculture, the investment in labor, buildings, land improvements, and machinery is relatively high in relation to the investment in the raw land itself. The rate of increasing intensity as one approaches the market point would directly reflect the locational advantage of sites close to market.

Secondly, rings or zones of different commodity production would tend to emerge around the market point. This is because transport costs vary from commodity to commodity. For example, the per pound cost of transporting eggs is greater than the cost of transporting wheat. So the producers having particularly high transport costs (producers of eggs, fresh milk, fresh fruits and vegetables) would tend to bid the highest for land and would locate in a ring just around the market point. Producers with somewhat lower transport costs (meat raisers or grain farmers) would locate a little farther out. And the producers with the lowest transport costs (wool growers) would tend to locate on the fringes of the system, and so on.

So much for the theory. But is it of any value in explaining the present-day agricultural patterns of developed countries? At this point, the reader is challenged to open a good economic atlas, such as the *Oxford Economic Atlas of the United States and Canada*. The reader can see for himself whether the theory is of any value or not. Of course, the reader must bear in mind that there are many market points, rather than just one, so he should particularly direct his attention to the principal market points in the United States, such as the great consuming population of our Atlantic Megalopolis. Further, in a real-world situation such as this, variations in soil fertility affect the pattern markedly. For example, the Appalachian Mountains disrupt the pattern. Likewise, decreasing intensity in production away from Megalopolis (for example, in the Great Plains) can be explained by dryness as well as by distance from market.

But in spite of such distortions, I think the reader will agree that intensity does tend to decrease away from major market points and that there are tendencies toward a zonation in commodities away from these points. In short, New Jersey's fame as a "garden state" and as an egg and dairy producer is in part a reflection of its location between New York and Philadelphia. Similarly, the relatively non-intensive agricultural production of Mississippi cannot all be blamed on the mistakes of lethargic plantation owners; in part the agricultural pattern of Mississippi is a reflection of its location with respect to markets.

But the reader will also note from the atlas that there are some highly significant exceptions to the pattern one would assume from the von Thunen formulation. The production of fruits and vegetables in many places such as California and Florida for *national* markets certainly does not fit the von Thunen ideas. Perhaps one might explain this purely and simply as a question of variations in soil fertility. Those places are well-known to have great climatic advantages. But the maps show other distortions less easily explainable in that way, for example, the various areas of intensive production scattered through parts of the Middle West and Mountain

West. Many of them are quite distant from major metropolitan areas. What of them? One must recall that the simple von Thunen formulation discussed here *assumed that transport costs were directly related to distance*, so that the greater the distance the greater the transport cost. Broadly speaking, this was the case before the Second Agglomerative Revolution.

But the great transport developments of the nineteenth century changed all that. There are great economies-of-scale in such forms of mass transport as railroads, large ships, and pipe lines. Thus, the transport costs *per ton-mile* tend to decrease with distance. A farmer one thousand miles from the market point normally pays higher transport costs than a farmer only one hundred miles away, but certainly not ten times as much. Furthermore, the reduction in organizational atomization discussed previously can allow the farmer to achieve economies-of-scale in such things as planting, cultivating, storing, grading, advertising, and so on. Through cooperatives, for example, farmers can jointly use facilities and thus cut costs. In certain cases, economies-of-scale in production combined with economies-of-scale in transport are enough to free the farmer from the tyranny of distance as visualized by von Thunen.

The contemporary agricultural map reflects both kinds of adjustment to the need for market accessibility. It seems likely that, in the long run, the second kind of adjustment may become more and more common although it is difficult to conceive of a world in which the former type of adjustment disappeared entirely.

Other Accessibility Costs

Before the Second Agglomerative Revolution, market accessibility was the only major accessibility cost faced by the farmer. But no more. The businesslike farmer today is much concerned with the accessibility costs for raw materials, labor, services, and agricultural news. Raw materials in agriculture? It sounds a little strange, doesn't it? Once the raw materials used by the farmer were all right there on the farm itself: sunlight, rain, fertilizers, and home-grown seed. So land itself was considered the principal factor in agricultural production. But today the businesslike farmer uses many raw materials from off his farm, often from places thousands of miles away: chemical fertilizers, insecticides, herbicides, electricity, liquid fuels, commercial seeds, supplementary irrigation, and so on. And so for labor. Once the labor used was resident on the farm or in an adjacent village. Today the farmer may use seasonal labor that migrates from job to job over wide regions. No matter how low the wages of seasonal workers may be, those wages must be high enough to compensate the worker for the time and cost of travel. Of course, some seasonal workers are paid well indeed, such as the men with combines who migrate from Texas to Canada annually, following the wheat harvest.

The importance of accessibility to services can be illustrated by the egg farming region of New Jersey. The egg "farms" are factory-like buildings housing the "machines" (the hens); feedstuffs are trucked in and eggs and litter are trucked out. The farmer is a manager who employs several workers in his "factory." He is too busy and too specialized to do everything himself. So he also relies on a whole complex of specialists from the surrounding community for special services: veterinarians, culling specialists, chick-raising specialists, egg-packaging specialists, feeding specialists, truckers, and so on. Such a service complex that grows up to support a specialized form of agriculture is analogous to the service clusters that emerge in the metropolis to support manufacturing. Indeed, the existence of such an egg-service complex in New Jersey is a major advantage for the industry there, perhaps even more important than nearness to major metropolitan markets. This is only an illustration; nearly all forms of businesslike farming have a great need for accessibility to services, and the emergence of service complexes helps to stabilize agricultural location, just as it does for manufacturing.

Accessibility to *appropriate* farm news is also highly important. For example, the radio stations of the Corn Belt carry detailed daily reports on the current market prices for pork and beef, major products of that belt, but they seldom quote prices for kumquats or peanuts! Generally, access to appropriate farm news is freest in areas already specializing in a particular kind of farm production. However, the large corporate farm can afford to maintain its own communication systems. Consequently, a farming corporation in Florida might have more direct links with potential supermarket customers in Cincinnati than would a small farmer on the outskirts. This may be a major factor in the weakening of traditional von Thunen rings of production around the metropolis. Taken together, the other accessibility costs often outweigh the single factor of distance from market. Indeed, in specific cases, any one of the other factors may outweigh market distance in importance for agricultural location.

Site Costs

The most important site cost for the farmer is land, right? Wrong! The average American farmer today spends more on machinery and other equipment than on any other site cost, including land. This is one of the major reasons that businesslike farming is coming to resemble manufacturing more and more. But whereas both farmer and manufacturer are concerned with substituting machinery for labor, the farmer is also concerned with using machines to modify the land, often in permanent ways. The modern farmer is a land sculptor, irrigating, draining, dredging, leveling, ridging, terracing, deep plowing, fertilizing, cultivating, and weed spraying as never before in history. In terms of the locational problem, this means that modern technology gives the farmer greater freedom in locational choice than ever before. Desirable natural qualities in the land are highly valued, now as in the past, but undesirable natural qualities can be overcome much more readily than before.

Yet land is immobile, and our modifications of it also acquire immobility. So land patterns still explain a great deal about the farmer's locational choices. Land prices reflect the accessibility of the land very closely. On the local level, land on a good paved highway is more expensive than land on a back road. On the regional level, land near Seattle is more expensive than land in the Palouse of eastern Washington, discounting variations in fertility. On the national level, farmland in Megalopolis or the Corn Belt is more expensive than land in Tennessee or Alaska. In short, the farmer has to "trade off" site costs against the need for accessibility in his particular type of farm operation.

This trade-off is made in the light of how much or how little the natural qualities of the land might help or hinder such a farm operation. Or, more accurately, how the farmer *thinks* they will. The more businesslike the farmer, the more likely this thinking is to be in an up-to-date scientific and engineering context. One aspect of such natural qualities as soil, climate, and topography is their relation to the *biological limits* for specific crops. For some crops, such as coconut palms, the climatic limits are quite restricted; but for other crops, such as wheat or potatoes, the climatic limits are quite wide. And so on. Generally, land that meets the minimal requirements for many important crops is more expensive because there is more competition for it. Land in the Great Valley of California or in the Corn Belt is a good example.

The production of a particular crop tends to be concentrated particularly within the *biologically optimum* areas for that crop, assuming accessibility factors are favorable and assuming there is not too much competition from other crops for which the area is optimal, too. However, there is nothing necessarily permanently fixed and immutable about either biological limits or biological optima. The biological limits for many domesticated crops were gradually increased as, century after century, the First Agglomerative Revolution spread northward in Europe. But whereas such adaptations were very gradual during the spread of the First Agglomerative Revolution around the world, they are often very rapid today. The Second Agglomerative Revolution has made the stretching of biological limits and the shifting of biologically optimal areas a subject for detailed laboratory research and practical field demonstration; hence changes are much more rapid in our time.

As a result, specific pieces of land can become productively *obsolescent* (that is, lose their optimality) through agricultural research, just as the machines of the manufacturer can become obsolescent through industrial research. Relatively rapid changes in the value of particular geographic areas for particular kinds of agricultural production are to be expected today. With these warnings in mind, the reader should now open a good atlas and compare the maps of climate, soil qualities, topography, and so on with the maps of agricultural production. He will note many significant correlations that are not readily explainable in terms of accessibility costs or other site costs. Except for the influences of earlier times (inertia in the system), these residuals represent basic influences of the qualities of the land itself *today*. Tomorrow, who knows?

Governmental Regulation of Agricultural Location

The new agricultural knowledge, the new technology, gives the farmer far greater freedom in locational choice than ever before. But today the farmer is allowed to exercise only a part of that freedom. His locational choices must be made within certain constraints laid down by national agricultural policy. Specific policies differ from country to country, but all developed countries restrict the farmer in locational choice, some quite markedly. Modern national governments are "hung up" on a great dilemma. On the one hand, they want all of the advantages of the new locational flexibility, including particularly lower prices. The decline in the cost of producing farm products in the last century has been remarkable and has made possible the trend toward a service-dominated metropolitan economy. Yet, on the other hand, the new locational flexibility is frightening, especially because whole regions might become depopulated as a result. If the agriculture of a particular area declines, then there may also be a sharp decline in the service employment and manufacturing employment of the same area, insofar as these were located there in the first place because of links with farm production or agricultural consuming populations. In America, in a generation or less, much of the land won by such long and patient toil by our ancestors, the way-of-life farmers, might become the habitat of the hoot owl and the hazelnut.

So, in all developed countries, there are restrictions on agricultural location. These are many and varied; it would take several volumes to even begin to explain the many locational implications of contemporary agricultural policies. But the most noteworthy single aspect, perhaps, is the use of *acreage controls* to limit and stabilize agricultural production. In the United States, the production patterns of the past (basically the geographic patterns of the 1920s and 1930s) are the base from which the policies operate. Thus, where there was wheat production then, there is usually wheat production now, although the percentage of a particular farm devoted to wheat may be less than before. And so on.

In short, there is a great deal of governmentally induced *inertia* in the contemporary locational patterns of American agriculture. At this point, the reader might do well to check this assertion by comparing maps of agricultural production of forty years ago with maps of similar production today. He would note that the inertial effects have been much greater for some crops than others. For example, the stabilizing effect of governmental policies is very marked for both wheat and tobacco. On the other hand, the location of cotton production has shifted very decidedly in the same period. At this point, the reader might want to review again the previously assumed correlations between agricultural location and such factors as climate, soil, and topography, and attribute some of this correlation to locational inertia induced by governmental policies. In general, there are many analogies between the zoning laws of the metropolis and the agricultural map as administered from Washington.

Agricultural Concentration in Metropolitan Interstices

Though the locational choices made by specific farmers must vary according to the balance of all the locational factors previously discussed and hence will vary for different kinds of farm production, the general result is toward location in *metropolitan interstices* and toward specialized *agricultural districts or regions* analogous to those discussed previously for manufacturing.

By metropolitan interstices, I mean the areas between or among metropolitan areas. Other things being equal, areas so situated are favored over more distant areas on the periphery of the main metropolitan system. Ease of accessibility to markets is only one reason for this. These areas tend also to have relatively easy access to raw materials and services. This is because these areas are closely tied to the manufacturing pattern and the general service pattern. Some of the raw materials and services used by farmers are unique to agriculture, but many of them are not. For example, the truck servicing needed by a farmer is not fundamentally different from the truck servicing needed by a wholesaler or manufacturer.

Of course, land peripheral to the metropolitan system would probably be cheaper. For historical reasons, as discussed in Chapter 2, most metropolitan areas are in places favorable to agriculture either now or in the past. So the land located peripherally to the system might be cheaper, but it would probably not be better in natural qualities or in land modifications favorable to contemporary production. The farmer locating peripherally to the system, as in Alaska, finds that "cheap" land is bought at the price of high accessibility costs, natural qualities of limited value, and high land-modification costs. A peripheral location is fine for a way-of-life farmer, but not for the businesslike farmer.

The attraction of the metropolitan interstices is further increased by a temporary imbalance between the amount of land actually needed for primary production and the total interstitial space available. The freeing of rural land from way-of-life uses by the accelerating agricultural productivity associated with the Second Agglomerative Revolution has occurred more rapidly than the loss of land to agriculture by the outward growth of the metropolis and by metropolitan demands for recreational spaces. At some time in the future, locations peripheral to the metropolitan system may again become attractive, particularly if the rate of increase in agricultural productivity slows down (it seems somewhat doubtful that the rates of the 1950s and 1960s can be long maintained) or the demand of metropolitans for space for non-agricultural land uses continues to increase. There is one significant exception to the attraction of the metropolitan interstices. This is the case of tropical plantations producing tropical and subtropical crops. Yet this appears to be of declining significance. It is discussed in Chapter 11.

The second general locational tendency is for the formation of agricultural regions and districts analogous to those of manufacturing within the metropolitan interstices. Some of these represent specialization in a particular product, such as spring wheat. Others are much more complex and are more analogous to industrial complexes such as the Iron-Steel Complex or a petrochemical complex. That is, the varied kinds of agricultural production within the region are functionally related to each other and hence mutually self-supporting.

Some aspects of Corn Belt agriculture are simply remnants of general farming such as that which prevailed in the "agriculture as a way of life" age. But other aspects of Corn Belt agriculture correspond more to the patterns of an industrial complex. For example, the old tendency for each individual farm to raise several crops and several kinds of animals is giving way to more specialization on each farm. In turn, there is intrabelt trade of various products within the Corn Belt, an overall regional agricultural complex rather than a complex confined to each farm as an entity. The egg region of New Jersey is another example of such an agricultural region, or the orange-beef cattle complex of Florida, to name but two. The stronger the functional linkages tying these regions together, the more agricultural production is stabilized geographically.

II: FORESTRY

Forestry of sorts began with the First Agglomerative Revolution. It was necessarily limited at first because the Middle East had only limited forests. But as the revolution spread, it developed particularly in the forested areas of Europe, China, and Southeast Asia. For long centuries, the clearing of land for agriculture went hand in hand with the production of lumber and wood for a variety of purposes. Patches of forest were retained as the agricultural frontier advanced, so that woodlands tended to be scattered all through the settled areas. Wood was considered a very valuable raw material, but it was too heavy in relation to its value to transport very far. So the settlement matrix of agriculture and a hierarchical system of village-town-city encompassed also forestry. As the First Agglomerative Revolution spread around the earth after the fifteenth century, similar patterns were established everywhere that trees grew naturally and in some places where they had to be planted by man. But this immemorial geographic association of forestry and agriculture began to break down in the nineteenth century.

For one thing, agricultural settlement outran the forested belts and extended into such grasslands as the Prairies of North America, the Steppes of Russia, and the Pampas of Argentina. The new technology (including such things as the six-gun, barbed wire, steel plow, well-drilling equipment, railroad, and so on) made it possible to develop the grasslands for commercial farming. The rise of forestry in *other* areas such as the Lakes States to supply these grassland areas with wood products also made this settlement possible. The geographic split between forestry and agriculture had begun.

For another thing, the emerging metropolitan economy had an almost insatiable appetite for wood and wood products. Many of the demands for wood or its products were basically new. Thus, though paper had been invented centuries earlier, it was the metropolitan economy that made use of paper on a grand scale. Who could imagine a modern metropolis without paper? For a time this demand could be met in association with clearing the land for agriculture, but soon most commercial forestry came to be concentrated in specialized regions. Often these were regions of doubtful agricultural potential peripheral to the emerging metropolitan system of production, such as the Pacific Northwest or the Great Lakes-St. Lawrence area of North America or the great taiga of Eurasia extending from Norway into Siberia. Or, on a lesser scale, they were in the metropolitan interstices, as in the American Southeast or the pine forests of Germany. Forestry also came to be *organizationally* separated from agriculture. Small farm wood lots still exist, but in most developed countries they do not account for much of the total production. Most forestry is controlled by large firms and/or governments.

The same least-cost considerations applicable to manufacturing or agricultural location seem to apply to forestry. Locating close to the market is sometimes important, but economies-of-scale generally make it possible to resolve the question of access to market in ways similar to those for distant agriculture. Access to raw materials, labor, services, and business news play their roles. Site costs are similar to those for agriculture. Since forestry and agriculture compete for the use of space, since the biological range of some trees exceeds that of most grain crops, and since other locational factors are similar, forestry *tends* to be crowded into the peripheral areas.

However, this geographic pattern may change. Forestry is becoming less extractive; "tree farming" is becoming more common. Among other things, this implies the application of modern biology to the business. For example, new varieties of trees are bred, just as new strains of grains are bred. This could increase the ability of forestry to compete for space in the metropolitan interstices, as it already seems to be doing in the American Southeast. Further, site costs in the metropolitan interstices can be reduced through various forms of subsidy (tax concessions, government ownership of the land, and so on) thus making such locations more attractive. As the demand for recreational space near metropolitan areas increases, such subsidies may become more common. Indeed, one can conceive of "forestry rings" of that subsidized sort around metropolitan areas in the future. But for the present, the balance of locational forces much favors locations peripheral to the main metropolitan economic system.

III: MINING AND QUARRYING

Nearly all forms of production are undergoing dramatic changes in their locational patterns in our time. But none has changed more dramatically than mining and quarrying. These are very old kinds of production, predating the First Agglomerative Revolution in rudimentary forms. Even a hunting and gathering economy requires tools and minerals to make them from (such as flint for arrowheads). Preagricultural economies had far-flung trade networks focusing on favorable mineral sites such as flint deposits or obsidian quarries. Of course, the number and quantity of minerals used increased during the First Agglomerative Revolution. But the demand for most minerals was not great in an economy based on agriculture and a network of villages, towns, and cities serving agriculture. With the exception of a few of the rarer minerals, this demand could be met from relatively small workings of near-surface deposits found in or near the settled agricultural areas. The nature of the economy set limits on mining and quarrying and simultaneously set the geographic framework within which nearly all of it was done.

But the Second Agglomerative Revolution was and is a *mineral revolution*, both in the sense of sharply accelerating mineral demand and in the sense of a whole new geographic pattern of production. Per capita consumption of minerals, particularly key ones such as iron, has become one of the more reliable indices of the level of economic development among countries and regions. When one thinks of the rising demand for minerals in recent times, one usually thinks first of the great use of metals and petroleum in manufactured products such as automobiles and refrigerators. Indeed, the rising consumption of such products, and their rapid obsolescence, is very important.

But this is just part of the increased demand. One of the major aspects of the concentration of people, particularly in great metropolitan areas, is that these concentrations are also physical agglomerations of stone, brick, concrete, steel, asphalt, and so on. The mud and thatch peasant huts of former times, widely dispersed over the land, are of declining importance in developed countries. Furthermore, an elaborate transportation and communications network is essential for a metropolitan economy. Such networks are physical agglomerations of great quantities of sand, gravel, clay, stone, steel, copper, aluminum, petroleum, and so on. Hence it is not surprising that the demand for minerals has accelerated more sharply than the demand for food. To meet this rising demand, mineral production has been transformed in many ways, including its geographic pattern.

Of all major forms of production, mineral production today is the least geographically inhibited. The quest for minerals is more truly global in scope than any other. It is less restricted climatically than either agriculture or forestry; mineral exploration and production now occur in every clime and every topographical setting. Though the choice of mining locations perforce involves consideration of the location of agriculture and the location of services and manufacturing, it is more geographically independent of the rest of the metropolitan system of production than any other. If a profitable mining site can be found within the metropolitan interstices, well and good. But if not, more distant sites are chosen. The metropolitan economy intrudes more decisively on the economies of the underdeveloped countries through its world-wide mineral exploitation patterns than in any other single way. It is particularly in the sense of minerals that the geographic reach of the metropolis can be said to be world-wide. Decisions among alternative mining sites are characteristically made within a global context rather than a more restricted regional or national context.

Though the arena of choice is global, the actual production of many, many minerals tends to be very highly concentrated geographically *at any one point in time*, concentrated in a few highly favorable areas. This agglomeration of mining from its formerly more widely dispersed pattern is a pronounced feature of the Second Agglomerative Revolution. But whereas some of the other agglomerative patterns, such as the concentrations of large numbers of people in metropolitan areas or the emergence of industrial complexes, seem to have considerable geographic stability and even permanence, the pattern in mineral geography is very flexible. For example, I would be willing to predict that the petroleum industry of 1990 will be highly concentrated, with a relatively few areas producing the bulk of the world's total production of crude oil. But just which areas or countries? That I would be less willing to hazard a guess about. Not surprisingly in an industry with such a global scope, large corporate organizations play a major role in mining, though there are also small mining and quarrying firms.

The least-cost approach previously used for manufacturing and for agriculture seems to be the best way to make sense out of present-day locational patterns in mineral production. Market accessibility varies in importance, being greatest for those minerals that are heavy in relation to their market value (for example, sand, gravel, stone, coal, petroleum) and least for those whose market value is high in relation to their weight (for example, diamonds, uranium, gold). Of course, between these extremes is a great range, occupied by the other minerals. Just as with agriculture, there are two major solutions to the market accessibility problem. One is to stress production *near* the market; this has a significant effect on the production of nearly all the heavier minerals, but particularly stone, clay, gravel, and sand. The production of these, and some portions of all mineral production, tends to be relatively near the metropolitan areas.

The other solution is to select sites advantageous for other reasons and to offset the distance to market problem by making use of economies-of-scale in transportation and in the actual production itself. This solution is common in many cases, including petroleum, sulphur, and bauxite. Other accessibility costs also tend to be least near the metropolitan areas. Modern mining requires a much greater variety of raw materials and services than the older forms of mining and these are obviously more freely available in the metropolitan interstices than in remote peripheral locations. Modern mining labor expects more in services than did miners of the past, so inducing labor to move to peripheral locations is expensive. However, as long as such services are provided and good wages paid, modern miners are more willing to move than the more locally-oriented miners of generations past. The problem of accessibility to business news and gossip can be resolved just as it is with the large organizations in manufacturing. That is, there is a geographic separation of the various levels of management, with top management usually located in one of the major metropolitan areas and the more routine management located with respect to other considerations. With the exception of business news, all of the accessibility costs tend to favor mining locations in the metropolitan interstices, though more for some minerals than others.

Then what of site costs? These vary geographically too. For example, though both taxes and land may be relatively cheap in northern Alaska, the costs of operating there day by day are bound to be higher than in less rigorous climates. Most of the site costs of mining are relatively obvious, but taxes, royalties, and exploration costs require some explanation. The question of probable taxes and royalties is very difficult for the miner to predict, especially if the site is in a foreign country. Host countries have a strong tendency to revise such payments upward *after* the mining firm has already made major investments in exploration, site improvements, and transport systems to carry labor, supplies, and services in and to carry the mineral out. Then it may be too late for the miner to resist such increased payments. However, the mining company can offset this somewhat by operating in many different countries, especially if it is a large, global corporation. The host country is less likely to raise taxes to ruinous levels if it knows that the mining firm has other geographic alternatives. In any case, the significance of this locational factor varies greatly from area to area and time to time.

The locational problem for mining differs from that for services, manufacturing, agriculture, and forestry in that exploration costs play a major role. These costs tend to increase over time, rather than to decrease, as more and more of the obvious near-surface deposits are worked out. Part of these costs are borne by governments, particularly in advanced countries. The preparation of detailed geologic surveys by government agencies became a widespread practice in the developed countries early in the Second Agglomerative Revolution; it is only recently that the governments of the less developed parts of the earth have seen the necessity for so doing. Consequently, the mineral resources of the developed countries are much better known than those of other countries. One should be highly suspicious of comparisons of mineral resources between a developed country and an underdeveloped country. The developed country is likely to *appear* better endowed; whether it actually is or not is not so easy to say without equally detailed surveys in both cases. The less developed countries now see the importance of detailed geologic surveys, but they often lack the financial and research resources to compete effectively with the developed countries in such survey work. So they are particularly favorable toward contractual arrangements with large, international mining concerns.

Even in developed countries, the increasingly technical nature of the work tends to give the advantage to the large concern. In short, there are economies-of-scale in mineral exploration, just as in so many other aspects of location. For its part, the mining firm is often willing to invest relatively large sums in mineral exploration, knowing that many specific ventures will not "pay off," but that the exploration endeavor as a whole probably will. The expansion in geologic knowledge and in mining engineering has been more rapid than the growth of demand for minerals. There is a temporary imbalance between the amount of known mineral-bearing land and the actual production required, a temporary imbalance somewhat similar to that found in agriculture. This gives greater flexibility in locational choice than ever before.

And it tends to put a premium on site considerations in deciding where to mine. Site considerations probably play a more important role in mining than in manufacturing, forestry, or agriculture. That is, site considerations are relatively more important in relation to accessibility considerations. But this is not necessarily a permanent condition. Of course, as long as much of the mineral requirements of the metropolitan economy are met from relatively small underdeveloped countries with unstable governments, the large international firms will be interested in further mineral exploration for political reasons as well as economic ones. That is, continuing exploration in many countries is a means of offsetting the dangers of expropriation or excessive taxation in any one specific country.

Mining location is affected by inertial factors as well as by the balance among the site costs and accessibility costs prevailing in the case of a particular mineral. Mining in the metropolitan interstices is favored because modern mining began there and because such areas are more adequately surveyed. But this advantage is waning as older deposits are mined out and especially as the great successes of modern exploration and economy-of-scale approaches to mining and transportation show the great mineral potential of the earth as a whole. So another inertial factor enters the picture.

Just as the governments of metropolitan economies have a dilemma in relation to agriculture, they also have one about minerals. They like the advantages of the new flexibilities in mining location, particularly the resulting lower prices of raw materials. But, on the other hand, rapid changes in the location of mineral production can be frightening and, sometimes, socially undesirable. The "cheapness" of imported minerals is sometimes bought at the price of creating a pocket of unemployable indigents on the dole in the former mining region. Hence the governments of most metropolitan economies now have some sort of locational regulations restricting mining, at least imports. Underdeveloped countries also seek to influence mining locations in a variety of ways. However, it is probably safe to assert that such "zoning" is less significant than that for such other forms of production as manufacturing or agriculture. Mining is relatively flexible and free in its choice of location.

The net effect of all these locational factors tends toward some degree of *metropolitan zonation* and, within such zones, the development of highly concentrated *regions* or *districts* of mineral production. By metropolitan zonation, I mean a three-step zonation something as follows. First, in the metropolitan interstices and relatively close to the metropolis, there is a tendency to concentrate mineral production, especially such minerals as sand, clay, gravel, and stone, but also others. Second, there is much varied mineral production in the metropolitan interstices generally. Third, the metropolitan economies reach out, increasingly, to the ends of the earth, to every climatic region and to the most remote places. This third ring of mineral development seems to be growing more rapidly in volume of production than the other two.

In the first ring, there are often relatively small workings. But in the second and third rings the general trend is toward the development of mining agglomerations. On a world scale, most of the production of a specific mineral may be concentrated in only a handful of such great regions. The location of these acquires some geographic stability because of the investments in fixed facilities and because of similar inertial factors, but on the whole the location of such regions tends to respond very rapidly to shifts in the locational balance. Hence, one should not necessarily expect great stability in the mining patterns shown in an atlas. Instead, one should review the pattern frequently as new maps are produced.

CHAPTER 10

Spatial Production Systems at the Supra-metropolitan Level

If the principal theme of preceding chapters is basically true, that a modern developed economy is essentially a metropolis expanded or a metropolis writ large, then the notions developed in Chapter 6 should have a counterpart here: if it is important to understand the economic geography of the metropolis as a total spatial system, then it is equally important to try to understand the economic geography of major economic regions, nations, and blocs of nations as integrated spatial wholes. Understanding Central Place networks, industrial regions, and agricultural regions by themselves is indeed meritorious, but this is only a beginning; we must also try to understand how such networks and regions fit together into an overall spatial framework of production.

And not just how they might fit together in a static way, at any one specific point in time, but also how they fit together in a dynamic way. Presumably, if there are advantages in understanding the metropolis as an *evolving spatial system,* ceaselessly shifting in its internal locational associations and ceaselessly expanding outward to take in new areas and places, then there would be advantages in viewing a greater economic area such as a large, developed nation in a similar fashion. And presumably, just as some parts of the metropolis may become relatively poorly integrated with the overall spatial system (for example, ghettos), so once well-integrated parts of a national system of production may, over time, become less well-integrated, resulting in much economic distress. Thus, depressed areas such as parts of Appalachia were once more closely linked with the main production system than they are today.

However, it is one thing to suggest such a way of interpreting the economic geography of a nation or of blocs of nations (such as the European Economic Community) and it is quite another to produce detailed spatial models of this type. The vision of contemporary economic geographers of this large universe beyond the metropolis tends to outrun their abilities at concrete description. It will probably be some time before economic geographers have experimented enough with alternative models of such phenomena that they can produce general models of wide applicability. Probably a variety of models at differing scales (degrees of generalization or complexity) will be needed. The discussion in the rest of this chapter is necessarily highly speculative and more suggestive than definitive.

The reader can gain some idea of what I am talking about by examining the maps of transportation and communication networks in a good modern atlas, particularly in relation to the discussion in preceding chapters and in relation to atlas maps of the production of services, manufacturing, agriculture, forestry, and mining. Some areas and places show up as very closely tied to the overall system, while others are only weakly linked or hardly linked at all.

But maps showing routes alone do not tell us how much actual movement there is over the routes, so many atlases now include also *flow maps*. Flow maps are attempts to show pictorially the variations in movement on different routes, usually by variations in color or width of line. They help a great deal in developing a broad understanding of modern economic geography. The flow maps found in atlases often include maps of population movement, analogous in certain respects to the commuter maps of the metropolis, but extending over longer time periods. There may also be flow maps of the movement of the major commodities, such as steel, petroleum, and wheat. Unfortunately, atlases seldom include maps of the movement of assembled items such as automobiles, or of service commodities such as investment funds, but in research studies nearly all aspects of economic geography have been shown at some time on flow maps.

Perhaps the most important single aspect of a modern economy is not the movement of commodities or established services, but rather the movement of ideas. The rate and direction of the *diffusion* (spread) of new forms of production or new forms of consumption through the whole spatial system is of great importance in the modification of present patterns and the emergence of new ones. Indeed, differences in the patterns of diffusion in developed and underdeveloped economies are probably the most crucial single geographic difference between them. But maps of such flows are still largely confined to research studies and do not ordinarily show up in atlases.

Flow maps do help to give a general idea of broad patterns. But their usefulness is severely limited by the great complexity of the phenomena involved. Even if one had flow maps of every single item relevant to the forms of production discussed in preceding chapters, one would not necessarily grasp it all. It is just too complex. There are limits to strictly visual understandings. Computer mapping, now in its infancy, may soon come to our aid. The data involved in the extraordinarily complex spatial linkages of a modern economy could be fed into a computer with great storage capacity. Then, computer maps could be produced at will to highlight the particular linkages under study at a specific moment. The computer is greatly reducing the historic difficulty of economic geography, the need to manipulate such great masses of locational data. In the past, economic geographers were kept so busy manipulating data that they did not have as much time as they needed to concentrate on actually explaining the locational patterns. Hence the following explanatory concepts are rather rudimentary in nature.

Though the *core-periphery* concept is rather rudimentary, it is nevertheless useful. Various writers describe an economic core area in the United States. Where and what is the core? If only one core is shown for the United States, its boundaries are usually relatively close to those of the historic manufacturing belt (see Chapter 8). But much more is implied in this case than a concentration of manufacturing. This area also includes much of the most productive agriculture in the United States, in part because of accessibility considerations (Chapter 9). It also has much mining, though only limited forestry. And it has a highly developed service complex going beyond that found in the usual metropolis or the towns and villages dependent on it; it includes services (such as those of government, education, corporate management, and banking) that exist only at a much more limited level beyond the core. In short, the core concept implies a highly integrated economy in which agriculture, services, and manufacturing are linked closely in a tight-knit spatial system.

If that is the core, then the rest of the United States is the periphery. For example, the Great Plains is in the periphery. The Great Plains is peripheral both geographically and economically. It is more dependent on the core than the core is on it because the production of the Great Plains is more specialized. Its main contribution to the system is in the agricultural sector, whereas the core has agriculture, manufacturing, and highly developed services. Similarly, the Rocky Mountain States are peripheral. And economically dependent. The Rocky Mountain States are very dependent on the core for tourists and for markets for mining, forestry, and agriculture. But the core sends its tourists to many other areas as well, and it derives raw materials from many other peripheral areas, too, some within the country and some abroad. Meanwhile, the Rocky Mountain States are dependent on other parts of the periphery as well as the core.

Of course, if the core-periphery concept is to be understood in these terms, then the core of the late nineteenth and early twentieth centuries, basically the historic Manufacturing Belt, must be supplemented by some lesser cores today. In short, today there are lesser cores on the West Coast, the Gulf Coast, and in the Southeast. But if one adds too many cores in an attempt to make the concept more viable, the looseness of the whole concept becomes evident.

Indeed, the core-periphery concept merges into the growth-point or growth-area concept. Sometimes a core is considered as more or less synonymous with a developed area, and a part of the periphery with an underdeveloped area. The core may be considered the principal agent of change in the system; it is often within it that production changes relevant to the whole system originate. Innovations in production are most likely to start there and then spread to the periphery. Hypothetically, the core might gradually expand so that all of the peripheral areas within a nation were included in it; the core would then be synonymous with the national boundaries and not be of much value in interpreting the spatial system. Or, the peripheral area might become dotted with lesser cores, which gradually merged with each other or with the principal core. Of course, if one identifies a very large number of lesser cores in the periphery then the concept merges with that of growth points discussed in Chapter 6. Whereas within a metropolis, a growth point might be just a few adjacent blocks, at this scale a growth point might be a metropolitan area, or more likely, a cluster of nearby metropolitan centers.

The core-periphery concept and the related growth-point idea do not allow for very precise measurement of the relationships among the different parts of a space economy. They are too general and basically nonquantitative. Therefore, many research workers are trying to develop more sophisticated modes of analysis. Such attempts include the *gravity model* and *maps of potential*. In a gravity model one ignores all the complex questions of human motivation discussed in earlier chapters and concentrates on simple and specific concepts derived from physics, such as mass, distance, direction, and velocity. For example, it can be assumed that the linkages between any two cities will be directly related to the size of their populations and the distance between them. To illustrate, consider three metropolitan areas—Cincinnati, Buffalo, and Minneapolis-St. Paul. Broad speaking, their populations are of the same size range. One would assume more linkages in both variety and volume between Cincinnati and Buffalo than between Cincinnati and Minneapolis-St. Paul. Why? Because of the relative distances involved. Now let us bring Chicago into the picture. According to the gravity idea, the linkages between Cincinnati and Chicago would exceed those between Cincinnati and Buffalo. Why? Partly because Chicago is closer to Cincinnati, to be sure. But primarily because the population mass of Chicago so much exceeds the population mass of Buffalo.

Of course, in actual studies, specific arithmetic formulas are used to derive the "pull" of one populated area on another. One can use such formulas to predict what the linkages or interaction between two or more cities ought to be, assuming the analogy to physics to be valid. If one lacks actual data on interactions one can substitute this assumed linkage. Or, if one has actual and precise data, one can compare the data with what would be expected according to the formula and use this to highlight those aspects of the relationship of the two cities that are relatively unusual.

If such gravity models are of value in studying the pattern of linkages between two cities, then why not more? Why not develop maps of a whole economic system such as a nation, maps that show the relative pull of all production points or consumption points on each other? This has been done, in *maps of potential.* Such maps show, by means of contour lines, the attraction of the various productive areas for each other and hence show the potential for movement of people or things among them. They do not show actual movement. Of course, gravity models or maps of potential need not be based on population alone. Instead, one can use per capita income or some other measure. The principal criticism of such approaches is that they can never produce more than a very general understanding of the overall spatial system of production. Analogies from physics can only take us a little way toward understanding. After that, we are still faced with the complexities of human motivations and human institutions.

Another approach used today is to apply mathematics and geometry in the interpretation of transportation and communications systems. Perhaps the best way to explain this would be to ask the reader to do some doodling. Take some paper and draw on it a map of a hypothetical country. On it put various dots and circles to represent the urban centers and/or production points. Now, then, draw lines to show the transport network linking these places together. How did you decide which places to link and which not to link? How did you decide which to link directly and which to link indirectly through other transport centers? If you started all over again would you create the same pattern and in the same sequence? Probably you drew the lines as you did at least in part based on some sort of notion of economizing or minimizing the number of linkages needed.

In studies of transport networks, geographers are trying to develop rather more sophisticated notions of just what we mean by "minimum distance." By developing hypothetical transport networks from such studies, one can see something of what is involved in the evolution of actual transport networks. By comparing hypothetical networks with actual networks, one can determine just what is most geographically significant about the actual pattern. And one can show that, at one particular stage of development, one transport pattern might emerge, but that at some later stage of development, this might decline in favor of a quite different geometric arrangement. Such analysis is helping to take away some of the mystery formerly associated with why a specific geographic area might blossom in one time period but decline in another.

A related approach is to stress the study of the *nodes* or junction points on a transport network. The idea here is to develop notions applicable to "systems of cities," whether the system is of a limited geographic scope, such as the cities of the Ruhr in Germany, or of a broader scope, such as the Megalopolis of the Atlantic Seaboard of the United States, or of a still broader geographic scope, such as the cities of the Atlantic Basin. Of course, the Central Place Systems described in Chapter 7 are "systems of cities." But, as currently developed, the Central Place idea applies directly only to services and does not include other parts of the economy such as manufacturing. It is widely realized today that we need also a broader concept of systems of cities that includes more of the whole economy. Of course progress in understanding transport networks will go hand in hand with better understanding of the nodes.

A real understanding of supra-metropolitan spatial production systems will also require us to learn more about the role of *feedback*. Feedback is information (about how the system is operating) that affects subsequent operation of the system. For example, in large metropolitan areas commuters traveling by auto listen to radio reports on which routes are most clogged and change their driving plans accordingly. Similar patterns operate beyond the metropolis. For example, if a vacationer learns that riots are occurring at his destination, a resort city, he may change his plans. Or, if a particular part of the country is becoming economically depressed, the national government may change its transport policies or subsidize production in that area or otherwise intervene to modify the geographic pattern as it would otherwise develop. Although the notion of such feedback is a rather simple one, we have only a limited understanding of how it operates geographically today. Just as the mental maps that the inhabitants have of their metropolis affect its development, the mental maps that most Americans have of the United States very much affect its geographic development.

Ultimately, we may be able to describe and interpret suprametropolitan spatial production systems with considerable accuracy, accuracy at least as great as we now have for metropolitan areas. Highly detailed and sophisticated models of such systems may be available to guide the lawmaker, the business decision-maker, and the professional planner. And more generalized but nonetheless basically accurate models of such systems may be available to the ordinary citizen to assist him in his role as a citizen and democratic decision-maker. In short, the spatial production systems of large economic areas may one day be quite comprehensible. But now we have only atlas maps, some tentative concepts, and some limited mathematical formulations to guide us.

PART IV

The Underdeveloped World

CHAPTER II

Locational Patterns in Underdeveloped Countries

Every book has its limitations as well as its advantages, and sometimes these are synonymous. This book's principal purpose is to provide a coherent view of the locational process and contemporary locational patterns. I have tried to do this by setting the locational discussion in the context of a revolution, the Second Agglomerative Revolution, by stressing the locational attributes of the most significant single expression of that revolution, the metropolis, and by tracing the emergence of similar patterns in areas far beyond the metropolis itself. This is advantageous in that it allows the reader to use his own observations, his own experience in rapidly changing locational reality to make some sense of the economic geography of our time. But this virtue is also a limitation.

Geographers since Hellenic times have tried to provide an understanding of the earth as a whole as well as in its parts. Indeed, the idea that the earth should be interpreted as a total system was one of the many major contributions of the Greek geographers. But the locational ideas stressed in most of this book apply in strength to only certain portions of the earth's area, to the parts already pervasively influenced by the Second Agglomerative Revolution. In short, to the so-called developed countries. Though the core of the developed zone still lies around the Atlantic Basin (the United States, Canada, Europe), the developed countries also include others somewhat more distant, such as the U.S.S.R. and Japan in the

Northern Hemisphere and Australia and New Zealand in the Southern Hemisphere. Beyond the developed zone there are still many millions of people and many millions of square miles as yet only partially touched by the Second Agglomerative Revolution. Such countries are generally called underdeveloped, developing, emerging, or by some adjective that will draw attention to their quite different economic patterns. Most of the countries in Asia, Latin America, and Africa are in this group. What kind of locational patterns do such countries or areas have?

Page limitations do not allow a very adequate answer to that question. The locational patterns differ *among* the underdeveloped countries as much or more than they do *between* the developed and the underdeveloped countries. There are very strong tendencies for particular locational patterns to repeat themselves with only minor variations in the developed countries because all such countries are being subjected to many of the same transforming forces, such as modern technology. But the underdeveloped countries have a great variety of locational forces operating in them. The spread of the First Agglomerative Revolution over the earth took many, many centuries, allowing many diverse variations on the main themes to emerge in relative isolation from each other. For example, the locational patterns of the Lake Zone in East Africa are very different from those of China. Further, there is great geographic variation in the underdeveloped world in the degree to which the Second Agglomerative Revolution has penetrated. In short, the locational patterns of the underdeveloped countries today have little unity and must be studied individually or in small groups to be understood in depth.

However, a few broad generalizations about the locational patterns of the underdeveloped countries can be made. The most important of these is that these countries characteristically have *dual economies*. One segment of the economy, usually the dominant segment, reflects traditional ways of production, including locational ways. The other and lesser segment of the economy reflects the ways of organizing things associated with the Second Agglomerative Revolution. Geographically, this means that it is the traditional locational framework that is the matrix or environment into which fragmentary pieces of a new and "alien" pattern have intruded. Sometimes it is illuminating to think of it in terms of two maps, one superimposed over the other. In large parts of the country the locational patterns derived from tradition show up very clearly, little affected by the intrusion. In a few parts of the country one sees patterns not too different from those found in developed countries. But in broad areas there is a confusing melange of the two patterns, confusing to "natives" and "foreigners" alike.

I: TRADITIONAL LOCATIONAL PATTERNS

Traditional locational patterns are dominated by the location of agriculture in its various forms (herding, shifting cultivation, intensive subsistence or peasant agriculture, and so on). Where agricultural populations are, there other economic activities tend to be also: forestry, mining, handicrafts, and services. Agricultural locations are the geographic key or framework for analyzing the whole economy. Therefore, to understand such a pattern one should not start with the major urban centers, as I did in Chapter 3. Instead, one should start with agriculture and proceed from it to an interpretation of services, handicrafts, and so on. The major traditional urban centers should be analyzed last, as a special expression of the agricultural environment in which they grew.

In turn, the whole context of locational decision-making in agriculture is quite different than it is in the case of the businesslike farmer discussed in Chapter 9. In the first place, the concept of the individualistic producer as a locational decision-maker is inappropriate. Individualism as a highly developed concept is a modern, Occidental idea. In these countries, *community* decision-making is dominant in most things, including locational decisions. And traditionally this community has been an immediate and local one such as a village, tribe, or extended family. Community locational decisions are informed and illuminated by the *culture*, by its values and its technology.

A very large portion of the agricultural production is food crops, so dietary preferences specific to that culture play a major role in the locational pattern of farming. The traditional technology severely limits locational choice because it generally does not permit extensive modification of the land in the short run. Of course, extensive terracing and similar investments in some areas show that peasant societies can greatly modify the earth in the long run. Since such communities live very close to the subsistence margin, the avoidance of risk in locational decision-making is more crucial than it is in more broadly based economies.

For these reasons, and closely related reasons, there is a very strong inertial aspect to the agricultural patterns. The agricultural population (and hence agricultural production) tends to be *where it has been*. It is quite erroneous to assume that the geographic distribution of the population today necessarily reflects an optimum distribution in relation to land qualities and contemporary opportunities. In many cases it does, but in other cases it does not. Generally, site considerations are more important than accessibility considerations, though it is the balance of all locational considerations that is crucial here, just as in the developed world.

Often, accessibility to market gives rise to a zonation of production around village or town market points, as one would expect from the von Thunen formulation (Chapter 9). Most commonly, the farming population resides in hamlets, villages, and towns, rather than on the land; as a result, other aspects of accessibility may produce zonations, too. For example, the intensity of production may gradually diminish in all directions from the village, in part because of rising commuting costs with distance. Who wants to walk farther and more often than he has to? Similarly, if the principal fertilizers used (human and animal wastes) are concentrated in the village, then they may be most freely applied nearest the village. For example, rings of especially productive land can often be noted around the villages of China. But however important accessibility aspects may be, they tend to be primarily rather local in their expression.

Site considerations, particularly those of climate, soil, and

Locational Patterns in Underdeveloped Countries / 191

terrain, are reflected on a broader geographic basis. Hence they are clearly evident on maps at the scale used in most atlases. At this point the reader should open a good atlas and note the many evident correlations between population distribution in underdeveloped countries and such natural features as climate and deltaic zones. Generally, such visual correlations are much more valid for underdeveloped countries than they are for developed countries. But even in this case, understanding in depth requires also a knowledge of the culture and history of the area.

As noted, the traditional locational pattern of agriculture is the basic geographic framework to which most other locations are related. Forestry is usually a small-scale enterprise, and often conducted in a widely dispersed pattern linked with agricultural enterprises. Mining, except for precious jewels and the like, is also primarily for local consumption and is similarly widely dispersed. If the rural population is relatively dense and relatively uniformly distributed over considerable area, then service patterns tend to resemble the Central Place Systems described in Chapter 7. But, of course with certain differences. There tends to be the same hierarchical overlapping of successively larger trading areas. But the lower portions of the hierarchy, the hamlets and villages, are usually proportionally more important. And the top of the hierarchy is represented by urban centers much smaller than the metropolitan areas of the developed world. Processing and fabricating are handicraft operations rather than manufacturing in the strict sense. Hence, rather than being highly agglomerated in industrial regions and the like, they are widely dispersed, generally in association with the Central Place pattern of services.

Various modifications away from these general service and handicraft patterns occur, of course, based on cultural differences, population density, and so on. For example, nomadic populations such as those of Morocco overcome the problems of range and threshold in services by holding periodic fairs. The fairs appear and disappear at established geographic sites according to principles analogous to those of more permanent Central Place Systems. In underdeveloped countries with histories of "civilization," such as those in West Africa, a relatively well-developed network of trails, roads, and rivers links all forms of production into an overall spatial system of production. However, such traditional spatial systems of production are usually relatively small in geographic scope compared with those of the developed world. The various parts or provinces of an underdeveloped country may have several small spatial production systems of this sort, only very tenuously linked together in a national system.

China is not a typical underdeveloped country in many respects, particularly in its very large population, its large area, and the relatively high level of spatial integration achieved before the great impact of the Second Agglomerative Revolution of the last century or so. Yet the case of China is instructive. Today, China is relatively poor and it is underdeveloped in terms of the norms of the Second Agglomerative Revolution. But it is important to realize that China is rather highly developed in terms of the norms of the First Agglomerative Revolution, more developed than much of the so-called underdeveloped world. And in the eighteenth century, before the Second Agglomerative Revolution had begun to transform the earth so markedly, China was probably the most developed large country on the earth.

Its agriculture was very productive, in harmony with Chinese dietary preferences and other cultural values, the agricultural technology of the day, and the qualities of the land itself. And China had a near monopoly on several agricultural products much desired in other countries (such as silk). This productivity was in part rooted in a locational pattern of agriculture that was appropriate for the First Agglomerative Revolution. Excessively destructive forestry had almost eliminated that activity from some areas, but bamboo raising flourished in conjunction with agriculture in the southern parts of the country. Though most production was for local consumption, there was also a significant interregional trade. For example, surplus rice produced in the Central Lake Region moved to the imperial court in Peking far to the north over a relatively elaborate network of waterways. Chinese ideas of political administration somewhat modified the sort of Central Place

System described in Chapters 2 and 7, but a broadly similar hierarchical pattern of hamlets, villages, towns, and cities covered the populated portions of the country. The distribution of handicrafts broadly followed this Central Place pattern, too, though there were some tendencies for regional specialization. A remarkable network of waterways and trails linked the whole production system together.

The economic geography of eighteenth century China was a wonder to the foreign travelers of that day. If the growth of population does not overwhelm China, then China may eventually become an economic wonder in terms of the norms of the Second Agglomerative Revolution too.

II: LOCATIONAL PATTERNS LINKED WITH THE SECOND AGGLOMERATIVE REVOLUTION

The effects of the Second Agglomerative Revolution on the underdeveloped countries have been very substantial, even though the economic geography of these countries tends to reflect the First Agglomerative Revolution more than the Second. For example, contact with the developed countries has encouraged a very rapid drop in death rates, while birth rates generally continue high. As a result, most of these countries are now experiencing a period of very rapid population growth. Since the traditional locational pattern developed in relation to a much smaller population, this often produces severe economic strains. Similarly, the ideas prevalent in the developed countries about the nature of man and his purposes (embodied in religion, government, science, and engineering) have had a shattering effect on the previously relatively stable cultures of the underdeveloped countries. Nearly everyone realizes that significant aspects of the old cultures are likely to pass away, but just what is to take their place is not yet clear. As a result of this confusion, political instability is common, with depressing effects on production. Making locational choices in such an unstable atmosphere is much more difficult than in the more stable economies of the developed world.

More specifically, there have been some modifications of the locational patterns of agriculture, forestry, mining, manufacturing, and services. Initially, these were particularly significant for agriculture. For example, the plantation system superseded previous patterns along the fringes of certain coasts and certain islands. Of course, the first plantations were not very scientific in their methods compared with the farming methods used in developed countries today. Yet they were an example of the trend toward businesslike farming discussed in Chapter 9.

Their operators (often a company rather than an individual) were more concerned with profits than with subsistence, though they often produced subsistence crops for their workers. The tendency to choose coastal sites reflected the fact that accessibility costs tended to outweigh size costs. The importance of plantations has declined somewhat in recent decades. But the production of several tropical crops such as bananas, coffee, tea, and rubber is most often on plantations. Many underdeveloped countries have no plantations today, or very few. But others, such as Ceylon, Brazil, Malaya, and Liberia, have their locational patterns much influenced by plantations. The survival of plantations is closely linked to the factors discussed in Chapter 9 for businesslike farming in developed countries. Many plantations are excellent examples of the great role of science and engineering in modern agriculture; and the role of large-scale organization, as in the case of the United Fruit Company. In some cases, peasant operators adjacent to plantations have begun producing export crops, too, taking advantage of such a location with its accessibility enhanced by the activities of the plantation itself.

Specialized crop regions have emerged in parts of some underdeveloped countries without taking the plantation form. In such cases, businessmen from the developed world have influenced locational choice primarily in the locations they have chosen for such services as the organization of trade. Because of high accessibility costs in relation to site costs, these are most often near the coasts. For example, most of the world's cocoa is produced in specialized districts in west Africa in a kind of partnership between small peasant producers and a large trading company from the developed world.

How long such modifications of the locational pattern of agriculture in the underdeveloped countries will continue to be of importance is not clear. For one thing, the accelerating population pressure generally means that the competition for land between local subsistence crops and export crops is growing keener. For another, the developed world appears to be growing less and less dependent on such areas as sources of agricultural raw materials. The recent very rapid increases in agricultural productivity within developed countries are a part of this; much of the agricultural trade of today is between developed countries rather than between developed and underdeveloped countries. In addition, the developed world has created substitutes for many agricultural products formerly produced solely or primarily in the underdeveloped world. A few examples will suffice: quinacrine for quinine, artificial rubber from petroleum for natural rubber, and artificial fibers from petroleum and coal for such natural fibers as cotton and jute. These are only examples; the list lengthens year by year.

Ultimately, the export of food from developed countries to underdeveloped countries may prove much more important in the locational patterns of those countries. For example, the distribution of United States shipments of wheat for famine relief in the great coastal metropolitan areas rising in India most certainly influences the overall locational pattern of India as well as the agricultural pattern. And, ultimately, the attempts of the underdeveloped countries to meet their developmental problems may well involve some copying of the plantation model for locational planning. For example, the ill-fated Chinese "Communes" were an attempt to develop a new locational pattern of production through large-scale organization more akin to plantations than the traditional peasant plots.

The impact of the new mining patterns has been much more marked. The impact of the accelerating demand for minerals in the metropolitan economy in recent decades on the locational patterns of the underdeveloped countries has been profound. And this impact appears to be increasing rather than decreasing. Most of the mining in the underdeveloped countries is carried on by mining companies based in the developed world or by domestic firms closely modeled on them. Thus, the locational choices are made in much the same way in both developed and underdeveloped countries. Of course, political factors play a more important role in foreign ventures than in domestic ventures, as discussed in Chapter 9.

But, in any case, the locational choices for mining are made with only partial reference to the traditional locational patterns of the underdeveloped countries. Very often, the mining districts are "islands" of development clearly reflecting the locational norms of the Second Agglomerative Revolution set in a "sea" of underdevelopment reflecting the norms of the First Agglomerative Revolution. Very often, too, these mining districts and the transport lines linking them to export points on the coasts are becoming growth points around which the economic geography of the country is being restructured. But in other cases, the environment of the mining district is so dry or otherwise inhospitable to the growth of agriculture, forestry, manufacturing, or services that little long-term growth potential exists in that part of the country. In such cases, the mining has only an indirect impact on the locational patterns of the country as a whole. For example, the tax money from the mining may be used to develop transport systems buttressing the traditional locational patterns of the country or it may be used to foster quite different patterns, for example, the growth of a very large metropolis such as the capital city.

Unless the developed countries turn to the oceans as a major source of minerals or unless they emphasize the mineral development of their own territories for largely political reasons (for example, American development of the Alaskan Arctic), we can expect that mining will continue to be one of the most important ways in which the developed countries transform the locational patterns of the underdeveloped world.

The political leadership of the underdeveloped countries

tends to be particularly conscious of its dependence on the developed world for manufactured articles. The traditional processing and fabricating of the underdeveloped countries, their traditional handicrafts, cannot compete very effectively. So they want to adopt the factory, one step in the process of agglomeration. But the small, isolated factory cannot compete very effectively either. The economic efficiency of the developed countries is based on much more than the concentration of production in large buildings (factories). As discussed in Chapter 8, the clustering of factories in metropolitan areas and in industrial complexes such as the Iron-Steel Complex of the United States produces savings in transport costs and in economies-of-scale. So if the underdeveloped countries are to compete, even in their own domestic markets, they must somehow move from a few factories (one has to start somewhere) to clusters of factories, to large metropolitan areas, to industrial districts and regions, and so on.

But doing this destroys the traditional locational pattern of the country. It starts the process of shifting from an economic geography rooted in peasant agriculture to an economic geography rooted in metropolitan systems of which agriculture is an appendage rather than the controlling element. Hence such a trend is a clear threat to the traditional culture, the traditional system of values. Much has been made of the lack of capital in underdeveloped countries with which to develop modern manufacturing. However, this *cultural* dilemma is actually more crucial. Each of the underdeveloped countries must decide for itself how much of its limited capital should be used to attempt to shore up a crumbling pattern of economic geography and how much should be used to develop bold new patterns reflecting the norms of the developed world.

Of course, some of the investment capital is from external sources, from the developed world. When the source of capital is private, as with branch plants of an American or European firm, the locational choice is guided by basically the same considerations prevailing in the developed world, that is, by the kinds of considerations discussed in Chapter 8. However, political factors rather similar to those discussed in

Chapter 9 for mining also influence locational choice markedly.

In most underdeveloped countries, the state greatly influences the choice of site. In addition to private sources of external capital, intergovernmental loans or grants are now an important source too. But whatever the source, the leaders of the state must resolve the cultural dilemma noted above. Much confusion in locational policy results. For example, to some extent India has tried to encourage locating factories where the people are; that is, they have sought to preserve the agricultural and village pattern. Yet, on the other hand, the government of India by a great diversity of acts has fostered also the breakdown of that pattern, the growth of specialized industrial districts and great metropolitan areas.

Most underdeveloped countries have a *partially developed* service network appropriate to the Second Agglomerative Revolution. That is, there are usually some hospitals, some modern schools and colleges, some banks of a modern type, and so on. But the overall service network is incomplete and fragmentary. For example, one may find a complete range of banking services in the capital city, but beyond that, little or nothing, no network of lesser banking cities or modern savings institutions in the countryside. In the chief port or the capital city, one may find a full range of all kinds of insurance, but beyond that city the only form of "insurance" may be that provided by the informal bonds of family, tribe, or village community. And so on for other services. The most complete range of services is likely to be found in the capital city, in major ports, and in other locations highly accessible to contacts with the developed world, though not necessarily highly accessible to most of the people of the country.

Perhaps the greatest impact of the developed world on the underdeveloped world has been in the growth of metropolitan areas, often one great metropolitan area out of proportion in size to the lesser urban centers of the country and out of all proportion to anything such countries have known in the past. The role of Bangkok in Thailand is an example. Often such a metropolis may have a very high proportion of the modern manufacturing and services of the country. And on its mar-

Locational Patterns in Underdeveloped Countries / 199

gins there may be most of the businesslike farming of the country. Such a center is a growth point around which the economy is transforming itself from the traditional pattern. But beyond it, the old patterns may persist with only slight alteration. Of course large countries such as India or China have several such metropolitan growth points.

Part of the swollen populations of such metropolitan areas may reflect desperation in the countryside more than the growth of employment opportunities in the metropolis. That is, in many underdeveloped countries, employment opportunities in manufacturing and services are not spreading throughout the country fast enough to absorb the population growth. Nor can agriculture, in its traditional locational pattern, absorb the added people. As a result, the landless from the countryside travel in desperation to the major metropolitan areas. These rural poor often form slum-like rings around the metropolis, in sharp contrast with the elegance of American metropolitan suburbs. They help to make the metropolitan areas of the underdeveloped world a rather different phenomenon from that generally associated with the Second Agglomerative Revolution.

III: THE FUTURE OF THE UNDERDEVELOPED COUNTRIES

It seems probable that the current confusing mixtures of the locational patterns of the past and the locational patterns induced by contact with the developed world will give way gradually to new patterns reflecting the triumph of the Second Agglomerative Revolution over all the earth. If there is to be peace, either within these countries or for the earth as a whole, contemporary locational instability cannot long continue. There seems little reason to believe that these countries can attain standards of living comparable to those of the developed countries without adopting locational patterns broadly resembling those described in the earlier chapters of this book.

Yet this resemblance need not mean slavish copying. It is

quite possible that some of the older locational ways indigenous to specific cultures will be able to survive in the long run through some blending of old ways and new or through some locational mutation not now foreseen. Such developments might then be adopted all over the world, as noted in Chapter 2. In short, it seems probable that at some time in the future, the economic geography of the whole earth will be organized on the basis of broadly similar locational ideas. But just how soon the old patterns will dissolve and new ones emerge is anyone's guess. Until this happens, economic geography will continue to be an ever-changing subject and hence a very stimulating inquiry to pursue. Who really wants to go back to the neat, orderly (and dull) geographic world of my grandmother? Who would really prefer locational equilibrium to the fascinating locational flux and change of our time?

Bibliography

Economic geography began to intellectually transform itself markedly after World War II, particularly after about 1955. The framework of ideas around which the field organized itself, the kinds of questions it posed, the ways in which these questions were posed, and the methods used for answering both new and old questions all began to change. Perhaps the most obvious characteristic of the "new geography" is its emphasis on theory and quantification, often to the irritation of geographers more wedded to the "old geography." But other changes are occurring, too.

Contemporary economic geography tends to stress locational questions of relevance in the here and now in the developed economies; it tends to draw back somewhat from the geographer's quest for global understanding to focus attention on the increasingly complex geographies of advanced nations. Topically, this means a preoccupation with the metropolis and urban systems generally (topics such as services, manufacturing, housing, agglomeration economies, urban and regional planning, and the like) to the neglect of topics that long dominated economic geography (agricultural regions, frontiers of settlement, conservation in rural areas, the relation of physical geography to economic geography, and so on).

The new geography stresses its affinity for related fields such as regional economics, regional science, urban ecology, and planning. Whereas the old economic geography was complementary to economics without cooperating much with it, the new geography readily and frankly borrows useful ideas from economics. Intellectual integration is replacing isolation. Contemporary economic geography emphasizes the development of ideas operationally useful in the world outside the classroom as well as within it. In short, economic geography is coming of age.

But geographers are still heavily map-oriented, despite their contemporary prowess with algebra, geometry, the computer, and satellite photography. Indeed, the transformation of economic geography involves a revolution in map making and atlases generally. The *Oxford Regional Economic Atlas: United States and Canada* (New York: Oxford University Press, 1967) illustrates this trend.

In such a time of rapid changes in ideas, the most relevant sources are the professional journals, particularly *Economic Geography, Geographical Analysis*, the *Annals* of the Association of American Geographers, the *Proceedings* of that association, and the journals of the Regional Science Association. Several excellent collections of articles have appeared, such as *Locational Analysis for Manufacturing* by Gerald Karaska and David Bramhall (Cambridge: M.I.T. Press, 1969).

Texts such as *The Geography of Economic Activity* by R. S. Thoman, E. C. Conkling, and M. E. Yeates (New York: McGraw-Hill, 1962) attempt to present both the old view of economic geography and the new, including some extended treatment of widely accepted new theories. But *A Preface to Economic Geography* by H. H. McCarty and J. B. Lindberg (Englewood Cliffs: Prentice-Hall, 1966) is labeled a "preface" out of confidence in the more theoretically oriented economic geography that is coming into being. The most advanced new text, almost a monograph, is Peter Haggett's *Locational Analysis in Human Geography* (New York: St. Martin's Press, 1966). Brian Berry's *Geography of Market Centers and Retail Distribution* (Englewood Cliffs: Prentice-Hall, 1967) will no doubt be followed by other text-level treatments of topics such as urban land use, transportation, wholesaling, international trade, energy, agriculture, and the like.

The greatest pioneer in the new geography was Walter Christaller, whose *Central Places in Southern Germany*, translated from the German by C. W. Basking (Englewood Cliffs: Prentice-Hall, 1966) reawakened interest in geography as geometry. Another pioneering work was Robert Dickinson's *City, Region, and Regionalism* (London: Routledge & Kegan Paul, Ltd., 1947); this was revised and published in 1964 as *City and Region*. Jean Gottmann's *Megalopolis* (New York: Twentieth Century Fund, 1961) is essential to the point of view in this primer. Many monographs reflecting the new geography are now coming out; Brian Berry's *Essays on Commodity Flows and the Spatial Structure of the Indian Economy* (Chicago: Department of Geography, University of Chicago, 1966) is an example.

The new geography is also "old" in the sense that many previously neglected authors have been rediscovered and reexamined, particularly Johann von Thunen, *Von Thunen's Isolated State*, translated by C. M. Wartenberg, edited by Peter Hall (New York: Pergamon Press, 1966), and Alfred Weber, *Theory of the Location of Industries*, translated by C. J. Friedrich (Chicago: University of Chicago Press, 1957).

The new geography actively relies upon ideas from more contemporary economists such as August Losch, *Economics of Location*, 2nd ed., translated by W. F. Stolper (New Haven: Yale University Press, 1954), E. M. Hoover, *Location Theory and the Shoe and Leather Industries* (Cambridge: Harvard University Press, 1937), and Walter Isard, *Location and Space-Economy* (Cambridge: M.I.T. Press, 1956), and on the work of sociologists such as Otis Duncan *et al.*, *Metropolis and Region* (Baltimore: Johns Hopkins Press, 1960).

Index

Accessibility costs: agriculture, 156–161; manufacturing, 62, 63–68; manufacturing beyond metropolis, 130–142

Agriculture: accessibility costs, 156–161; beginning of, 16; concentration in metropolitan interstices, 164–166; differences in location, 152–156; estate farming, 83; geographic crop production, 155; government regulation of location, 163–164; land ownership attitudes, 153; locational linkage between city and, 17–18; markets, 156–159; organizational atomization of, 153–154; perishable commodities, 82; population density and, 19–20, 24, 25; primary production and, 80–83, 150–166; separation from forestry, 168; similarities in location, 156; site costs, 161–163; specialization, 152–153; underdeveloped countries, 190–191; von Thunen model, 5–6

Albania, 118
American Revolution, 16
Appalachia, 4, 84, 101, 132
Arkansas, 134
Atlanta, 119–120
Australia, 11, 35, 127, 188
Automobile industry, 136–137; 153
Aztec Indians, 25

Bangkok, Thailand, 198–199
Berry, Brian, 111, 112, 114
Brazil, 127, 194
Buffalo, New York, 133, 180, 181

Canada, 11, 35, 127, 187
Celtic peoples, 37–38
Central Business District (CBD), 33, 47, 49, 54–55; urban renewal, 57–58
Central Business Office Complex (CBOC), 55
Central Government Complex (CGC), 55
Central Place Systems, 48–50; competitiveness and, 53–54; hierarchy, 50; meaning of, 48; Middle West, 111–112; range of, 49; threshold of, 49–50
Chicago, 20, 43, 77, 119, 130, 133, 142, 180, 181
China, 10, 11, 16, 23, 39, 118, 119, 188, 192–193
Cincinnati, 44, 89, 115, 120, 133, 180, 181
Cities: agriculture location and, 17–18; growth of, 21–22; Middle Ages, 22, 23
Cleveland, 44, 119–120, 133
Columbus, Christopher, 24
Community decision-making, 189
Competitiveness, Central Place Systems and, 53–54
Concentric ring model (spatial production system), 95–98; central point of, 96; criticism of, 96
Core-periphery concept, 178–181
Council Bluffs, Iowa, 111–112, 113
Cultural resistance, 37–39

206 / Index

Da Gama, Vasco, 24
Dairy farming, 131–132
Dayton, Ohio, 120
De Gaulle, Charles, 118
Detroit, 44, 133
Directional inertia, concept of, 99
Dutch Hollow (Cincinnati), 89

Economies-of-scale, 20–21; service economy, 45–46; transportation, 32
Egypt, 10, 11, 23
Estate farming, 83
European Economic Community (EEC), 118, 119, 177

Federal Reserve System, 117, 120
First Agglomerative Revolution, 11, 33, 35, 36, 110–111, 162, 166, 188, 196; beginning of, 25–26; cultural resistance, 37–38; meaning of, 8; Mesopotamian society, 16–18; resistance to, 37–38
Flow maps, 177–178
Focality, role of, 20
Ford, Henry, 136
Forestry, 166–168; separation from agriculture, 168; underdeveloped countries, 191
French Revolution, 7

Gary, Indiana, 132, 133
Geography of Market Centers and Retail Distributions (Berry), 114
Germany, 33, 182
Ghana, 134
Great Britain, 33, 118
Greece, 23

Harris and Ullman model, 101
Historical perspective, 15–39; introduction to, 7–12
Houston, Texas, 44
Hoyt, Homer, 98, 99

Inca Empire, 16
India, 10, 11, 16, 195
Indonesia, 10
Industrial Revolution, 27, 29
Iraq, 8

Iron-steel complex, 133–135, 144, 197
Italy, 23, 34

Japan, 23, 35, 126, 127, 187–188

La Crosse, Wisconsin, 131
Labor, division of, 20
Land speculation, primary production and, 87–88
Leningrad, U.S.S.R., 119
Liberia, 194
Locational inertia, role of, 35, 36
Locational patterns: equilibrium, 8, 27; Europeanization of, 25–26; introduction to, 3–14; *see also* types of patterns
London, England, 26–27, 44, 118, 119
Los Angeles, 44, 110
Louisiana, 132

Malaya, 194
Malthus, Thomas R., 25
Manufacturing (location), 4, 5–6, 60–75; accessibility costs, 62, 63–68; Central Business District, 72–73; cost factors, 62–74; decision for, 61–62; general clusterings, 64; industrial complex, 64; least cost, 62; manufacturing districts, 71–74; market outlets, 64–65; metropolitan area, 60–75; metropolitan services, 67; near employee residences, 66–67; public attitudes and, 60–61; site costs, 62, 69–71; suburban clusters, 73–74; summary, 74–75; tax considerations, 69, 70–71, 74; zoning regulation of, 61
Manufacturing beyond metropolis, 125–148; accessibility costs, 130–142; business news and gossip, 141–142; government regulation of location, 143–144; interpreting map of U.S., 146–148; labor costs, 139–141; markets, 135–138; metropolis as manufacturing mirror, 129–130; national level locational factors,

Manufacturing beyond metropolis (*continued*) 144–145; raw material costs, 130–135; site costs, 142
Market outlets, location of, 64–65
Marshall Plan, 136
Megalopolitan area, meaning of, 15, 43
Mesopotamia, 8, 16–18, 19, 25, 33, 35, 39; division of labor, 17; economies-of-scale, 21; limits to agglomerative growth, 21–22; resource conversion, 18
Metropolis, 43–103; manufacturing, 60–75; meaning of, 43–44; primary production, 76–91; services in, 43–59; spatial production system, 92–103
Middle Ages, 22, 23
Middle West hinterland, 110–115; Central Place System, 111–112
Michigan, 126, 136
Milan, Italy, 44, 119
Milwaukee, Wisconsin, 131
Mineral Revolution, 27, 29
Mining industry: primary production and, 83–85, 169–175; underdeveloped countries, 195–196
Minneapolis, 44, 131, 180
Montreal, Canada, 110
Morocco, 191
Moscow, U.S.S.R., 118

New Jersey, 82–83
New York, 32, 43, 44, 82, 109, 123, 137–138, 139, 142; Central Place System, 50; manufacturing, 65–66; population, 20; primary production, 77; service network, 117–118
New Zealand, 11, 35, 188

Occupational shifts, 30–31
Ohio, 44, 89, 115, 119–120, 132, 133, 180, 181
Omaha, Nebraska, 111–112, 113
Oslo, Norway, 119
Oxford Economic Atlas of the United States and Canada, 146, 150, 158

Pakistan, 23

Paraguay, 11
Paris, France, 118–119, 123
Philadelphia, 44, 82, 120
Pittsburgh, 110, 120
Plantation system, 194
Population: agriculture, density and, 19–20, 24, 25; Malthus on, 24
Primary production, 76–91; agriculture and, 80–83, 150–166; attracting forces, 79, 80–85; beyond fringes of metropolis, 77, 149–175; equilibrium, 88–90; forestry, 166–168; land speculation, 87–88; locational patterns, 77–78; long range, 85; metropolitan area, 76–91; mining industry, 83–85, 169–175; nature of, 76–80; repelling forces, 79–80, 85–88; resolution of attraction and repulsion, 88–91; short range, 85; taxation and, 79, 85; transportation and communication, 87; wage rates, 85; zoning and, 79
Production system: division of labor, 17; economies-of-scale, 20–21; forms of, 9–10; horizontal interpretation of, 12; primary, 76–91, 149–175; Second Agglomerative Revolution, 29–32; social order, 10–11; spatial, 92–103

Quarrying, 169–175
Quebec, 132
Quinacrine, 195

Raw materials, distribution of, 130–135
Regional shopping areas, 47
Renaissance, 33
Resource conversion, 18
Rome, Italy, 23, 24, 119

St. Louis, 119–120
Science, technological changes and, 27
Seattle, 120
Second Agglomerative Revolution, 14, 27, 109, 118, 124, 150, 196; beginning of, 33; cultural re-

Second Agglomerative Revolution (*continued*)
sistance to, 38–39; effects on underdeveloped countries, 193–199; geographic advance of, 33–34; meaning of, 7–12; occupational shifts, 30–31; production process, 29–32; resource-converting technology, 28–29; space-adjusting technology, 32–33; transitional period to, 24–25
Sector model (Hoyt model), 98–102
Service network: beyond metropolis, 107–124; Central Business Office Complex (CBOC), 55; Central Government Complex (CGC), 55; Central Place Systems (CPS), 55; complexities, 50–55; conflicts and compromise, 46–47; contemporary changes, 55–59; customer and, 45–46; economies-of-scale, 45–46; general case pattern, 45–50; geographic changes, 55–59; higher order goods, 47; in hinterlands, 109–115; hypothetical metropolis background, 44–45; lower order goods, 47, 59; medical, 53; metropolitan area, 43–59; 115–124; patterns of, 45–59; retail distribution, 47–48; specialized functional areas, 53, 54–55; underdeveloped countries, 198; urban renewal, 58; wholesaling, 51–52
Site costs: agriculture, 161–163; manufacturing, 62, 69–74; manufacturing beyond metropolis, 142
Slums, 66, 101
Space-adjusting technology, 18–19, 25, 26, 32–33; innovations in, 32
Spatial production system: beyond the models, 102–103; concentric ring model, 95–98; core-periphery concept, 178–181; maps of potential, 181–182; metropolitan area, 92–103; multiple nuclei model, 99–102; nodes on transport network, 182; role of feedback, 182–183; role of perception, 102–103; sector (Hoyt) model, 98–102; self-regulation, 93; supra-metropolitan level, 176–183; underdeveloped countries, 191–192; Urban Data Banks, 94, 103
Stockholm, Sweden, 119
Supernaturalism, 27, 28
Switzerland, 33

Taxes, primary production and, 79, 85
Texas, 132
Thailand, 198–199
Tocqueville, Alexis de, 8

Uganda, 11
Underdeveloped countries, 11–12, 14, 35; agriculture, 190–191; community locational decisions, 189; forestry, 191; future of, 199–200; locational patterns, 187–200; political leadership of, 196–197; Second Agglomerative Revolution and, 189–199; service network, 198; spatial production systems, 191–192; traditional patterns, 189–193
Union of Soviet Socialist Republics (U.S.S.R.), 23, 35, 118, 119, 127, 187–188
Urban Data Banks, 94, 103
Urban renewal, 57–58

Von Thunen model, 5–6, 95, 156–157

West Virginia, 132
Wisconsin, 131, 133

Yugoslavia, 118

Zoning laws, 61, 143–144; primary production and, 79

About the Author

===

ROBERT B. McNEE, Professor of Geography at the University of Cincinnati, is one of the foremost economic geographers in the country, and has published numerous articles in scholarly journals. A former Fulbright Fellow, he received his B.A. from Wayne State University, his Ph.D. from Syracuse University, and has taught at the City College of New York, Southern Illinois University, and Wayne State. He has traveled extensively throughout the United States and the world, from Big Timber, Montana, where he was born, to 45 of the 50 states, the Soviet Union, Western Europe, the Mediterranean countries, East Asia, and the Pacific Islands.